The Aspirational
Investor

The Aspirational Investor

Taming the Markets to Achieve Your Life's Goals

ASHVIN B. CHHABRA

HARPER
BUSINESS

An Imprint of HarperCollins*Publishers*

THE ASPIRATIONAL INVESTOR. Copyright © 2015 by Ashvin B. Chhabra. All rights reserved. Printed in the United States of America. No part of this book may be used or reproduced in any manner whatsoever without written permission except in the case of brief quotations embodied in critical articles and reviews. For information, address HarperCollins Publishers, 195 Broadway, New York, NY 10007.

HarperCollins books may be purchased for educational, business, or sales promotional use. For information, please e-mail the Special Markets Department at SPsales@harpercollins.com.

FIRST EDITION

Designed by Renato Stanisic
Illustrations and figures designed by Accurat (www.accurat.it)

Library of Congress Cataloging-in-Publication Data has been applied for.

ISBN: 978-0-06-223509-1

15 16 17 18 19 OV/RRD 10 9 8 7 6 5 4 3 2 1

For Daniela

I have lived a charmed life since the day I met you

Acknowledgments

Inasmuch as this book is not just about the subject of investing, but an attempt to elucidate an entirely new framework for how people should connect their goals and aspirations with their investments, *The Aspirational Investor* has been a work in progress for more than a decade.

I would like to start by thanking my two longtime collaborators, Ravindra Koneru and Lex Zaharoff. My thinking has benefited in innumerable ways from our conversations and collaborations.

This book is an evolution of my earlier paper "Beyond Markowitz." Strong support and encouragement for the work came early on from many, including Harry Markowitz himself; Bruce Greenwald, professor at Columbia University and "guru to Wall Street gurus"; Charlotte Beyer, founder of the Institute for Private Investors; Jean Brunel, fellow practitioner and editor of the *Journal of Wealth Management*.

I have learned from so many people at Merrill Lynch, as the firm, clients, and financial advisors adopted various aspects of this new approach. I must thank Andy Sieg, who brought me back to Merrill to complete an unfinished journey, as well as John Hogarty and John Thiel. The backing of the big three, together with David Darnell's enthusiastic support, made it evident that we were going to change the world of wealth management.

My six-year stint at the Institute for Advanced Study brought me back in touch with my scientific roots and matured me as an investor. The greatest influence was the chair of my investment committee, Jim Simons. Six years of closely working with a gentle and ever generous genius has got to take you to a whole other level! A number of distinguished committee members were generous with their wisdom and helped shape my investment philosophy, notably Marty Leibowitz and Nancy Peretsman. Others, including Victoria Bjorklund, Neil Chriss, Robbert Dijkgraaf, Roger Ferguson, Robert Fernholz, Peter Goddard, David Marquardt, Eric Maskin, David Rubenstein, Eric Schmidt, Charles Simonyi, Peter Svennilson, Shelby White, and Brian Wruble, kept me on my toes.

The accomplished group of ex-GS women partners, known as the Circle Financial Group, was another set of early adopters that provided valuable feedback, in particular Ann Kaplan and Jacki Zehner. I am also grateful to Charlie Henneman, Julie Hammond, and Rebecca Fender for a series of invitations from the CFA Institute to elaborate on the Wealth Allocation Framework.

Thank you also, Erin Bellissimo, Stacey Gaine, Lisa Grossman Hirscheimer, Samir Kabbaj, Michael Karam, Kristi Kuechler, David Laster, Richard Marston, Sandra Sanchez, Nick Stonestreet, and Nevenka Vrdoljak. This list of names (and no doubt I have left out many) does not do each of you justice in recognizing valuable contributions ranging from reference checks and error spotting to valuable discussions that ensured that the refinement of the framework would continue.

Freeman Dyson at the institute introduced me to the Brockmans. Thank you, Max Brockman: you have been the perfect agent!

My editor and publisher, Hollis Heimbouch at Harper, took a chance on a different kind of popular finance book and pushed me to find "my voice." Thank you for your patience as years went by and for turning on the right amount of pressure to get the job done!

Perhaps not surprisingly, much more was required to get to a finished book—Len Costa was my editor through the many drafts over several years! Ever patient and professional, through the combination of his sharp pen and deep understanding of the subject matter, he has brought not only clarity but a reader's perspective.

As I searched for an illustrator who would bring these ideas to life, I was lucky to find, quite by accident, the talented Italian firm Accurat. Thank you, Gabriele Rossi, Giorgia Lupi, Marco Bernardi, and Marwa Boukarim for your enthusiasm, creativity, and collaboration.

I grew up in a family of journalists and publishers, so perhaps it was inevitable that I would write a book. My mother has writer's blood in her veins. My sister Sagari set the standard early on for the next generation. Thank you, Mom and Dad, for creating a wonderful home where one grew up *aspiring* to change the world.

My wife, Daniela, unrelenting in her pursuit of clarity of thought and writing when I was willing to throw in the towel, worked with me on every aspect of this book. My daughter, Maya, who at an early age is already an editor's editor, helped by editing several chapters, while my son, Sasha, was ever willing to oppose all of my ideas, thus providing an effective counterpoint.

Lastly to you, the reader, thank you for reading this book. I hope it will have a lasting and positive impact well beyond your financial life!

CONTENTS

Introduction 1

PEOPLE

CHAPTER 1   The Investor's Worst Enemy 9

CHAPTER 2   The Psychology of Risk and Reward 21

MARKETS

CHAPTER 3   The Volatility of Markets over a Human Lifetime 31

CHAPTER 4   Speculative Bubbles and Market Manias 43

WEALTH

CHAPTER 5   How Do People Become (Very) Wealthy? 57

CHAPTER 6   How Much (Money) Do I Need? 73

A NEW FRAMEWORK

CHAPTER 7   The Wealth Allocation Framework 87

CHAPTER 8   Digging Deeper 101

OBJECTIVE-DRIVEN INVESTING

CHAPTER 9   Seven Steps to Implementation 121

CHAPTER 10 Owning the World 139

ASPIRE!

CHAPTER 11 Do Not Try This at Home 159

CHAPTER 12 The Aspirational Society 183

Notes 189

Index 211

The Aspirational Investor

Introduction

Money will not buy you happiness, but wealth does provide safety and comfort and, more important, it creates choices and opportunities. Whether your goal is to grow your wealth or simply to preserve it, how wisely you invest your assets will play a significant role in the quality of the life that you and your loved ones will lead.

Unfortunately, most investors, even those who are otherwise smart and successful, lack a basic understanding of financial markets. This causes them to make poor investment decisions. The problem is compounded by the fact that a great majority of us either do not realize our incompetence in financial matters or are simply unwilling to admit that it has a negative impact on our relationships and personal life.

Many investors do recognize their limitations and hand their money over to a professional advisor. Yet the process of delegating to a professional is fraught with peril. Most individuals have little understanding of what can (and cannot) be achieved through investing. After suffering through a major market disaster, such as the Great Crash of 2008, irate investors will fire their advisors and find someone else.

In the next market downturn, the cycle repeats.

The investment world has hardly helped matters. Despite more than sixty years of debate and research, academics and the financial services industry alike remain divided into two broad camps: the so-called *efficient market camp*, which holds that most investment managers simply cannot outperform the market, especially after taxes and fees are paid, and offers index investing as a prescription; and the *active management camp*, which seduces investors by pointing to track records of extraordinarily successful investors like Warren Buffett.

The average investor's results turn out to be quite dismal. Their portfolios under-perform not only the standard market benchmarks but also the individual funds they are invested in. We will explore this sad finding in detail.

The exciting and comparatively new field of behavioral finance highlights the role of psychology and emotion in investing. So far, however, research in that field has uncovered a lengthy list of psychological biases that lead many of us down a faulty path, but it offers little insight as to why these "mistakes" are so persistent and hard to correct.

Meanwhile, the 24/7 news cycle and the plethora of financial news websites mean that even casual viewers are constantly updated on every world event, big or small, and its supposed impact on financial markets. This abundance of information and analysis serves to alternately entertain and confuse, amplifying the noise and adding yet another barrier to sound financial decision making.

No wonder investors seem to lack the tools to succeed.

Your financial advisor may well be compounding the problem. If you work with a professional on a regular basis, chances are your meetings are animated by a variety of full-color graphics: pie charts detailing the allocation of your liquid assets and different ways to measure performance. The central focus is likely to be your returns over the past few quarters or the most recent calendar year. Time and again, the conversation with your financial advisor probably focuses on the investments that did well, the fund managers that under-performed and may need to be fired, and other changes to make based on predictions about what the investment climate might look like over the next few years.

So what's wrong with this picture?

The problem is that this focus on liquid investable assets that, by the way, may account for only a portion of your total net worth and (short-term) investment performance, anchors the traditional advisory relationship to the wrong set of questions. The emphasis becomes "How can I increase my returns or consistently beat the market?" instead of "How can I achieve my major life goals with some degree of certainty?"

In this book, I will argue that the grand debates in finance, particularly the clash between indexing and active management, are focused on a series of false choices. If the markets don't really care about you, as they surely do not, why should you spend all your time and effort trying to beat them? You certainly do not want the great successes of your life to be dependent on the future performance of financial markets.

And what about those so-called behavioral "mistakes"? Perhaps they are not errors at all. As we shall see, concentration and leverage—two of the biggest mistakes in finance theory—turn out to be the building blocks of substantial personal wealth for many entrepreneurial people. When smart and successful individuals constantly violate what seem to be straightforward guidelines of sound investing, such as diversification, there is clearly something more to the picture.

This book offers an entirely new approach to managing wealth—one based not on the markets but on achieving personal goals and carefully managing risks. The approach, which I call the *Wealth Allocation Framework*, begins with the idea that a truly comprehensive wealth management strategy must accommodate the dual need for financial safety and wealth creation, while also enabling you to maintain your standard of living through measured exposure to financial markets. The primary focus is around defining your personal objectives and then optimizing your financial assets and your human capital, or earning potential, around those objectives.

Conventional portfolio theory, ironically called *modern portfolio theory*, is a theory about optimizing risk and return from financial markets through optimal portfolio construction. What is needed is a theory that shifts the focus from portfolios and markets to individuals and objectives. I call this more useful and contemporary approach *objective portfolio theory*.

Intuitively, this *objective-driven approach* makes sense. We no longer live in a world of bountiful social safety nets, so exposing your entire net worth to the risk from financial markets in a quest for outsized returns is hardly a sensible strategy for achieving what is important in your life. Pensions and defined-benefit plans seem headed for extinction, and the future of Social Security benefits in their current form is in doubt. Secure company pensions have given way to the 401(k), which shifts the risk of running out of money from companies and the public sector to individuals. The traditional company job for life no longer exists. People are starting work much later, and living longer, at a time when health care costs continue to skyrocket. The reality is that, for most people, personal financial assets are no longer a supplement to a pension but represent everything they will have to live on.

Today all of us bear the burden of investing wisely. The demands on your portfolio will surely increase over time, yet you must be able to sustain your living standard and meet your financial obligations *throughout your lifetime and likely long retirement, regardless of prevailing market conditions.* Too much volatility at the wrong time can sink your strategy, unless you've properly insulated yourself against the whims of the financial markets.

Still, managing investments isn't just about financial safety. Attaining substantial wealth or creating a lasting impact often requires aspiring to lofty goals while managing and mitigating multiple risks. Whether it's launching a new business, holding on to a large, single-stock position, or investing in a promising project, there should be a place in your portfolio to pursue your aspirational ventures without jeopardizing your financial security. For many people, especially those with entrepreneurial leanings, a life of ignoring aspirations can be unfulfilling or, shall we say, filled with "aspirational regret."

The Wealth Allocation Framework is designed to accommodate the three seemingly incompatible objectives that should underpin every wealth management plan. The first is the need for financial security in the face of known and unknowable risks. The second is the need to maintain your living standard in the face of inflation and longevity. Third, but not last, is the need to pursue aspirational goals, be it for personal wealth creation, to create positive impact, or to leave a legacy.

I make the case for the new framework in the first four sections of this book. In "People," I examine the role of individuals, who, as noted earlier, are often their own worst enemies when it comes to investing wisely. Why do people throw good money after bad, regardless of whether markets are going up or down? Next, in "Markets," I tackle the volatile history of financial markets, which, contrary to popular belief, are often unstable even over long time periods, especially the most important one: a human lifetime. That helps explain why markets alone are not the answer to your investment strategy. In the section titled "Wealth," I'll review some surprising facts about how some people become very wealthy (hint: by breaking the "rules" of investing). Then I turn to the age-old question "How much money do I need?" and offer some practical strategies to help you identify, prioritize, and quantify your financial goals.

I then outline the Wealth Allocation Framework and explain how it connects your priorities with your current and future net worth, enabling you to build an investment strategy that helps you achieve your goals and aspirations. In the final section of the book, I reinterpret the strategies of two masters, value investor Warren Buffett and David Swensen, chief investment officer of the Yale University endowment, who pioneered the Endowment model. Examining their investment strategies through the lens of the Wealth Allocation Framework provides key insights into the strengths and weaknesses of each approach and the lessons for individual investors.

I conclude by examining the role of aspirational goals and aspirational investments in our lives and portfolios. While neglected by modern portfolio theory, our aspirations often embody what we live for, what drives and inspires us.

The book in your hands is a practical guide to a new approach to investing. If I've done my job properly, it will set you on a path to a more confident and fulfilling financial life.

PEOPLE

The Investor's Worst Enemy

What if I told you that you were unnecessarily giving up as much as two thirds of your investment returns? Your first impulse might be to blame inflation or the tax authorities. But inflation in the United States has averaged only about 3 percent annually over the last thirty years, and most market investments do keep pace with inflation. The highest long-term capital gains rate for investments held longer than a year is 20 percent. Any tax that claimed as much as two thirds of investors' returns would surely shut down the capital markets. So where does the blame lie?

What if I told you that you are both the victim and the culprit?

Every year, Dalbar, a respected research firm, analyzes in detail the returns individuals earn from their mutual fund investments. They then compare these returns to both market index returns and the returns from the funds the investors were actually invested in. No matter how you look at it, the results are not encouraging.

In the thirty-year period from 1984 to 2013, the broad-based Standard & Poor's 500 index delivered a very healthy annualized return of 11.1 percent. Over the same period, equity fund investors earned a paltry 3.7 percent per year, about one third of the index return. Bond fund investors fared even worse: with the Barclays Aggregate Bond Index returning an annualized 7.7 percent, individual investors captured just 0.7 percent (not a misprint!) in annualized returns. Inflation annualized at 2.8 percent during that period, which means that the average investor's return on a balanced portfolio, consisting of 60 percent equities and 40 percent bonds, did not even keep up with inflation. That staggering underperformance is the cost that individual investors paid for following their instincts on adding or pulling money out of their funds (often at the wrong time) or for staying out of the market while it enjoyed an upswing. Retail investors, they found, under-performed both market indices and the very funds they were invested in.

Statistics like these can lead to plenty of hand wringing—and denial. Many investors look at their own returns with an air of resignation. "It's not me. It's the markets." Most investors, however, hold the mistaken opinion that their own returns were slightly above average or much better than they actually were.

Consider, by way of analogy, this simple question: What kind of driver are you? It turns out that in almost any group, a large number of people identify themselves as above average. In Sweden, where an early systematic study of this simple question was conducted, between 70 percent and 80 percent identified themselves as above-average drivers. In the United States, a country whose citizens are known for their optimism (at least about their own abilities), approximately 88 percent identified themselves as "above average." In a good sample, though, only 50 percent of drivers would be correctly identified as above average. Clearly, when it comes to the very definition of "average," our self-perception is not particularly accurate.

This *illusion of superiority* is widespread and holds across a wide variety of human endeavors, including investing. It was studied intensively by two Cornell University researchers, Justin Kruger and David Dunning, who found that this illusion comes with an interesting twist. Somewhat ironically, the most incompetent people in the group often rate themselves the *highest*. That crazy driver, speeding and weaving across lanes, thinks his driving abilities are superior to yours! This is an everyday example of the Dunning-Kruger effect.

Alas, investors are no better at trading stocks. In the '80s advances in technology created user-friendly, scalable trading platforms. This allowed discount brokerage firms to offer self-directed online trading capabilities to retail investors. Not surprisingly, investors confident in their own trading abilities were early adopters. While financial firms loathe parting with investor data, two particularly persuasive University of California professors, Brad Barber and Terry Odean, were able to get their hands on the trading records of ten thousand anonymous, self-directed investors from a prominent brokerage house. Their work focused on trades conducted over a seven-year period (1987 to 1993) in which an individual sold one security and bought another on the same day. Then they analyzed whether or not, one year later, the stocks that investors bought had outperformed the ones they had sold.

Why is this method of analyzing the trades so clever? Because when you trade one security for another, the wisdom of the transaction does not depend on whether the market as a whole subsequently goes up or down; all that matters is whether, a year later, the stock you bought went up *more* than the stock you sold. The resulting profit or loss number is a clear and simple way of quantifying the profitability, and wisdom, of these trading decisions, irrespective of how the market as a whole performed.

The title of the paper, "The Courage of Misguided Convictions," is a dead giveaway for the dismal results: in most cases, over the following year, the stocks that investors bought under-performed the ones that they sold—by a lot. The average return was roughly a *9 percent loss per trade*. Not surprisingly, Odean and Barber's follow-up paper was called "Trading Is Hazardous to Your Wealth."

The unfortunate truth is this: whether it comes to mutual fund investing or buying and selling stocks, individual investors have a propensity to make frequent, ill-timed, and costly trading decisions.

In other words, all too often, investors are their own worst enemies.

Still, active management is a zero-sum game, and there exists another set of market players that seems to make money fairly consistently: leading institutional investors and a highly skilled subset of other professional investors, including Wall Street trading desks and upper quartile mutual and hedge fund managers. How much of their success is passed on to you, the individual investor, if you are lucky enough to invest with them?

The answer is: not that much. Yale professor Roger Ibbotson and his collaborators Peng Chen and Kevin Zhu have documented this unfortunate finding. They analyzed mutual fund and hedge fund performance from 1995 to 2009, compared it to the returns from investing passively in an index, and found that the excess returns over a benchmark generated by the typical mutual fund manager were roughly equivalent to the fees they charged. In other words, even when individual investors aren't themselves trading indiscriminately, mutual funds *on average* provided investors *with no incremental return* after accounting for fees. Hedge funds, during that time period, delivered respectable outperformance of about 6.8 percent a year on average. However, this result came at a hefty price: more than half of the excess return was lost to fees, leaving an actual excess annual return of about 3 percent. Fast-forward to 2013, and we find that the out-performance of hedge funds over mutual funds has reversed post-2008. Most hedge funds lost more money in the 2008 crisis than expected, and, since then, those that have maintained some degree of hedging or reduced market exposure have found it difficult to match the returns of buoyant post-crash markets.

The upshot? Even when you pick professional money managers, there's a strong chance that you would end up relinquishing a large part of your investment profits to fees, while, of course, solely bearing the risk of any losses. That's not exactly an attractive value proposition, as succinctly expressed by Charles Ellis in his influential and insightful 1975 article "The Loser's Game."

Such disappointing results provide numerical context for the life's work of eminent Princeton economist Burton Malkiel. After many decades of careful research, Malkiel concluded that the vast majority of money managers simply couldn't beat the markets over the long run. His evidence and conclusions are published in a book that first appeared in 1973, called *A Random Walk Down Wall Street*, which has sold more than a million copies and is widely recognized as an investment classic.

Malkiel's view combines the teachings of *modern portfolio theory*, a foundational model in finance, which holds that there is an optimal mix of asset classes for a desired level of risk, and the *efficient markets hypothesis*, which holds that securities' prices reflect all (or most) known information, thus making it impossible to consistently beat the market.

His simple proposal: figure out your tolerance to risk and identify an optimal asset allocation. Then, instead of looking for top money managers or trying to play the market yourself, simply buy index funds that broadly represent each asset class in your portfolio.

For example, if your risk appetite leads you to a portfolio consisting of 60 percent stocks, 30 percent bonds, and 10 percent cash, you could allocate 60 percent of your portfolio to a low-cost equity index (e.g., the S&P 500 index or, better yet, a world equity index), 30 percent to a bond index (e.g., the Barclays Capital Aggregate Bond index), and put 10 percent cash in the bank.

Two years after Malkiel's book first appeared, investing gadfly Jack Bogle launched a new kind of money management firm based on the same premise. Bogle credits another prominent academic, Nobel laureate Paul Samuelson, for playing a major role in "precipitating the creation of the world's first index fund." Bogle gave investors a way to buy and hold the entire market, or pieces of it, through inexpensive predetermined indices. Today, the firm he founded, The Vanguard Group, is one of the leading purveyors of passive index investment products and ranks among the largest money management firms in the world, with more than a trillion dollars in assets. Vanguard's analysis seems to show that, with low fees and a simple approach, their index funds consistently beat most active money managers over the long haul. These numbers, they claim, are even more impressive when adjusted for the impact of taxes.

Malkiel and Bogle's approach, though compelling and easy to implement, provides an incomplete picture of the investing landscape. The fact is, some successful investors deliver consistently stellar returns by *concentrating*, not diversifying (much less indexing), their portfolios. One of the most famous, of course, is Warren Buffett. The chairman, CEO, and top shareholder of Berkshire Hathaway has delivered returns averaging close to 20 percent annually since 1968, beating the return on any equity index by a wide margin. A dollar invested in the S&P 500 in 1968 would be worth $59 today, while a dollar invested in Berkshire stock over the same time period would be worth a cool $6,540. For several decades, through Berkshire's annual shareholder letters, Buffett has shared his profound insights on the discipline of buying great businesses at the right price (read substantial discount), an investing strategy known as value investing. When Buffett likes a company, he buys as much of it as he can—in fact, he often snaps up the entire company—and then holds on to it. In many cases, he has no intention of selling.

George Soros, the hedge fund speculator extraordinaire, would certainly agree with Buffett's views on the limitations of diversification. Soros is famous—and in some circles infamous—for his massive bets across multiple asset classes based on macroeconomic trends, such as his fund's 1992 wager against the British pound. Being right on that single trade netted Soros and his investors a billion dollars.

While these two legendary investors may have very different ways of looking at and investing in the financial markets, they share a common belief in conducting careful research and taking big, concentrated bets that express their convictions. Their approaches, at least at first glance, run counter to the principles of asset allocation and diversification. As we shall see in the later chapters, so do the investment approaches of almost all families that have built great fortunes.

The upshot is that money managers, on average, fail to outperform the market, but some money managers do outperform, even over long periods. It is for this reason the world of investing remains divided into two warring factions: the *efficient market camp*, which holds fast to the data showing that most active managers add little to no value, especially after you account for fees and taxes; and the *active management camp*, which points to the likes of Buffett and Soros as proof that consistent outperformance is certainly possible and cannot be attributed to luck alone.

For proponents of efficient markets, the evidence overwhelmingly points to the high cost and futility of average retail investors trying to beat the market. The best investment strategy, this reasoning goes, is to diversify widely and implement an investment plan using low-cost index funds. This message is perhaps hard to swallow: "The best you can be is average—like everyone else." Yet, as we have seen, the empirical evidence is compelling.

Conversely, active management adherents fervently believe that skilled managers can beat the market over sustained periods of time, and sometimes by wide margins. They feel it is dismissive, even insulting, to attribute Buffett's great wealth and impressive track record to luck. They also point to the fact that the market is a zero-sum game, so investors with skill and discipline will systematically earn money at the expense of those who are not so talented. Indeed, the dismal performance of most individual investors supports this point.

One of the most entertaining ways in which this debate has played out unfolded on the pages of the *Wall Street Journal*, which, inspired by Malkiel's work, ran a competition pitting active managers against dart throwers.

At least twice a year, from 1988 to 2002, the *Journal* recruited four leading stock pickers to suffer the potential humiliation. The result? The long track record showed professional stock pickers beating the dart throwers 61 percent of the time. But, inexplicably, the contest design had a deep flaw: it did not take into account dividends being paid out by various stocks. This led the professionals to game the system by choosing stocks that did not pay dividends, while the dart throwers were, by design, blissfully unaware of this flaw. A correction—by reinvesting dividends paid out—would have shrunk the money managers' lead. And although the professionals beat the dart throwers 61 percent of the time and garnered a higher return, they beat the index itself only 53 percent of the time: their victory had a margin so narrow that, from the statistical point of view, it fell within the range of pure chance.

The efficient markets camp pointed out yet another problem with the contest: much like in the real market, the game itself was influencing the result. Interested *Journal* readers were buying the stocks picked by the professionals after reading about them in the *Journal*. This demand caused the stock picks to rise in price, thus providing the professionals with excess return completely unrelated to their actual stock-picking prowess. The excess return did not last, however. An analysis of the subsequent long-term performance of those stocks showed that, immediately after publication, the professional stock picks had a short bump in price that then diminished over time, and the stocks collectively ended up underperforming the index. Thus, retail investors imitating the stock selections of the professionals once again ended up worse off than either group.

A better design, apart from incorporating the effect of dividends, would have been to hold the entire contest in secret and announce the final results at the end of the agreed time period. But that design would have lacked the excitement of a real-time contest and probably sold far fewer copies of the newspaper. Ultimately, after fourteen long years, the *Journal* abandoned the contest without declaring a winner, satisfying neither side.

What's fascinating here is not which camp won or lost but rather the mere fact that pitting dart throwers against professional stock pickers was even a meaningful competition. Would a similar contest questioning the utility of other professionals, such as doctors or engineers, endure for fourteen years and finish so inconclusively?

In the end, great entertainment is too hard to pass up. Catering to the illusions and aspirations of individual investors, the *Journal* continued the portion of the contest that pitted dart throwers against *Journal* readers. More than a decade later, in April 2013, the *Journal* ended that contest with the darts decisively beating the *Journal* readers 30 to 19 over forty-nine contests. The *Journal*'s final word: "We are winding down the print-only version of the Dartboard contest and have introduced a more dynamic online version of the contest with our colleagues at MarketWatch." The games must go on!

The downside of great entertainment is that it can distract us from what really matters. Amid the perennial debate between the *efficient markets* camp and *active management* proponents—an important one, no doubt—a fundamental idea has gotten lost: investing should not be about "beating the market" but rather about achieving your goals with a reasonable degree of certainty. The Wealth Allocation Framework can help you refocus your investing activities on more practical and productive outcomes.

To understand the power of the approach, we must first explore why it is the case that so many investors, despite their best intentions, end up going so far astray when they hitch their fortunes to the financial markets.

2

The Psychology of Risk and Reward

Most of us have a healthy understanding of risk in the short term. When crossing the street, for example, you would no doubt speed up to avoid an oncoming car that suddenly rounds the corner. Humans are wired to survive: it's a basic instinct that takes command almost instantly, enabling our brains to resolve ambiguity quickly so that we can take decisive action in the face of a threat.

The impulse to resolve ambiguity manifests itself in many ways and in many contexts, even those less fraught with danger. Glance at the adjacent picture (Figure 2.1) for no more than a couple of seconds. What do you see?

Some observers perceive the profile of a young woman with flowing hair, an elegant dress, and

Figure 2.1: Anonymous German postcard (1888)

a bonnet. Others see the image of a woman stooped in old age with a wart on her large nose. Still others—in the gifted minority—are able to see both of the images simultaneously.

What is interesting about this illusion is that our brains instantly decide what image we are looking at, based on our first glance. If your initial glance was toward the vertical profile on the left-hand side, you were all but destined to see the image of the elegant young woman: it was just a matter of your brain interpreting every line in the picture according to the mental image that you already formed, even though each line can be interpreted in two different ways. Conversely, if your first glance fell on the central dark horizontal line that emphasizes the mouth and chin, your brain quickly formed an image of the older woman.

Regardless of your interpretation, your brain wasn't confused. It simply decided what the picture was and filled in the missing pieces. Your brain resolved ambiguity and extracted order from conflicting information.

What does this have to do with investing? Much like the lines in the image, every event and piece of information relevant to the financial markets can be interpreted differently according to your perspective. Does new data inform us about near-term risk or herald long-term return potential? For some, a 10 percent drop in the stock market is a strong signal to head for the exit. For others, it's a chance to snap up bargains.

Every trade has a seller and a buyer: your state of mind is paramount. If you are in a risk-averse mental framework, then you are likely to interpret a further fall in stocks as additional confirmation of your sell bias. If instead your framework is positive, you will interpret the same event as a buying opportunity.

The challenge of investing is compounded by the fact that our brains, which excel at resolving ambiguity in the face of a threat, are less well equipped to navigate the long term intelligently. Since none of us can predict the future, successful investing requires planning and discipline.

Unfortunately, when reason is in apparent conflict with our instincts—about markets or a "hot stock," for example—it is our instincts that typically prevail. Our "reptilian brain" wins out over our "rational brain," as it so often does in other facets of our lives. And as we have seen, investors trade too frequently, and often at the wrong time.

One way our brains resolve conflicting information is to seek out safety in numbers. In the animal kingdom, this is called "moving with the herd," and it serves a very important purpose: helping to ensure survival. Just as a buffalo will try to stay with the herd in order to minimize its individual vulnerability to predators, we tend to feel safer and more confident investing alongside equally bullish investors in a rising market, and we tend to sell when everyone around us is doing the same. Even the so-called smart money falls prey to a herd mentality: one study, aptly titled "Thy Neighbor's Portfolio," found that professional mutual fund managers were more likely to buy or sell a particular stock if other managers in the same city were also buying or selling.

This comfort is costly. The surge in buying activity and the resulting bullish sentiment is self-reinforcing, propelling markets to react even faster. That leads to overvaluation and the inevitable crash when sentiment reverses. As we shall see, such booms and busts are characteristic of all financial markets, regardless of size, location, or even the era in which they exist.

Even though the role of instinct and human emotions in driving speculative bubbles has been well documented in popular books, newspapers, and magazines for hundreds of years, these factors were virtually ignored in conventional financial and economic models until the 1970s.

This is especially surprising given that, in 1951, a young PhD student from the University of Chicago, Harry Markowitz, published two very important papers. The first, entitled "Portfolio Selection," published in the *Journal of Finance*, led to the creation of what we call *modern portfolio theory*, together with the widespread adoption of its important ideas such as asset allocation and diversification. It earned Harry Markowitz a Nobel Prize in Economics. The second paper, entitled "The Utility of Wealth" and published in the prestigious *Journal of Political Economy*, was about the propensity of people to hold insurance (safety) and to buy lottery tickets at the same time. It delved deeper into the psychological aspects of investing but was largely forgotten for decades.

The field of behavioral finance really came into its own through the pioneering work of two academic psychologists, Amos Tversky and Daniel Kahneman, who challenged conventional wisdom about how people make decisions involving risk. Their work garnered Kahneman the Nobel Prize in Economics in 2002. Behavioral finance and neuroeconomics are relatively new fields of study that seek to identify and understand human behavior and decision making with regard to choices involving trade-offs between risk and reward. Of particular interest are the human biases that prevent individuals from making fully rational financial decisions in the face of uncertainty.

As behavioral economists have documented, our propensity for herd behavior is just the tip of the iceberg. Kahneman and Tversky, for example, showed that people who were asked to choose between a certain loss and a gamble, in which they could either lose more money or break even, would tend to choose the double down (that is, gamble to avoid the prospect of losses), a behavior the authors called "loss aversion." Building on this work, Hersh Shefrin and Meir Statman, professors at the University of Santa Clara Leavey School of Business, have linked the propensity for *loss aversion* to investors' tendency to hold losing investments too long and to sell winners too soon. They called this bias the *disposition effect*.

The lengthy list of behaviorally driven market effects often converge in an investor's tale of woe. *Overconfidence* causes investors to hold concentrated portfolios and to trade excessively, behaviors that can destroy wealth. The *illusion of control* causes investors to overestimate the probability of success and underestimate risk because of familiarity—for example, causing investors to hold too much employer stock in their 401(k) plans, resulting in under-diversification. *Cognitive dissonance* causes us to ignore evidence that is contrary to our opinions, leading to myopic investing behavior. And the *representativeness bias* leads investors to assess risk and return based on superficial characteristics—for example, by assuming that shares of companies that make products you like are good investments.

Several other key behavioral biases come into play in the realm of investing. *Framing* can cause investors to make a decision based on how the question is worded and the choices presented. *Anchoring* often leads investors to unconsciously create a reference point, say for securities prices, and then adjust decisions or expectations with respect to that anchor. This bias might impede your ability to sell a losing stock, for example, in the false hope that you can earn your money back. Similarly, the *endowment bias* might lead you to overvalue a stock that you own and thus hold on to the position too long. And *regret aversion* may lead you to avoid taking a tough action for fear that it will turn out badly. This can lead to decision paralysis in the wake of a market crash, even though, statistically, it is a good buying opportunity.

Behavioral finance has generated plenty of debate. Some observers have hailed the field as revolutionary; others bemoan the discipline's seeming lack of a transcendent, unifying theory. This much is clear: behavioral finance treats biases as mistakes that, in academic parlance, prevent investors from thinking "rationally" and cause them to hold "suboptimal" portfolios.

But is that really true? In investing, as in life, the answer is more complex than it appears. Effective decision making requires us to balance our "reptilian brain," which governs instinctive thinking, with our "rational brain," which is responsible for strategic thinking. Instinct must integrate with experience.

Put another way, behavioral biases are nothing more than a series of complex trade-offs between risk and reward. When the stock market is taking off, for example, a failure to rebalance by selling winners is considered a mistake. The same goes for a failure to add to a position in a plummeting market. That's because conventional finance theory assumes markets to be inherently stable, or "mean-reverting," so most deviations from the historical rate of return are viewed as fluctuations that will revert to the mean, or self-correct, over time.

But what if a precipitous market drop is slicing into your peace of mind, affecting your sleep, your relationships, and your professional life? What if that assumption about markets reverting to the mean doesn't hold true and you cannot afford to hold on for an extended period of time? In both cases, it might just be "rational" to sell and accept your losses precisely when investment theory says you should be buying. A concentrated bet might also make sense, if you possess the skill or knowledge to exploit an opportunity that others might not see, even if it flies in the face of conventional diversification principles.

Of course, the time to create decision rules for extreme market scenarios and concentrated bets is when you are building your investment strategy, not in the middle of a market crisis or at the moment a high-risk, high-reward opportunity from a former business partner lands on your desk and gives you an adrenaline jolt. A disciplined process for managing risk in relation to a clear set of goals will enable you to use the insights offered by behavioral finance to your advantage, rather than fall prey to the common pitfalls. This is one of the central insights of the Wealth Allocation Framework. But before we can put these insights to practical use, we need to understand the true nature of financial markets.

MARKETS

10,000   200   50

3

The Volatility of Markets over
a Human Lifetime

Over the last five hundred years, the fortunes of mankind have improved immeasurably. In the agrarian age, the size of a country's economy was directly proportional to its population. To guess which economies were dominant in the agricultural era, we can simply look to the two most populous countries in the world today to come up with the correct answer: China and India, which flourished in comparison to England. But the emergence of the Industrial Revolution in the 1760s created a new model for productivity driven by the use of fossil fuel–powered machines. The countries that could successfully exploit the new model were prosperous on the economic front, as well as militarily dominant. The big winners of the Industrial Revolution were, of course, the British, the dominant superpower of the nineteenth and early part of the twentieth centuries, and eventually the Americans.

While the agrarian society dominated for more than ten thousand years, the Industrial Revolution was just a couple of hundred years old when, starting in the 1950s, it began to give way to the third important revolution, the digital revolution. At the crux of this revolution is the computer, a universal machine. All of us will be affected by the digital revolution, which offers exciting new opportunities but also creates large displacements, upending the old and accepted in the pursuit of progress.

Today, thanks to relative peace and modern medicine, many of us will live to be centenarians. All of us hope that we will be comfortable and happy in our old age, surrounded by people we love and not lacking any basic necessities. In fact, recent research indicates that happiness and contentment increase with age. Such optimism is predicated on our ability to save and invest wisely throughout our lives, so that our resources do not run out during our lifetime, leaving us dependent on others. That's why it is critically important to understand what we can reasonably expect from the financial markets over the time period that matters most: a human lifetime.

The episodes of modern world history are not for the faint of heart. The twentieth century saw famine and hyperinflation, genocide, communism and fascism, two world wars, and a nuclear-tinged cold war. Humanity has paid dearly in blood and treasure for its folly. These bleaker periods of history serve as a stark reminder that risk over long periods of time, from a century to even just a couple of decades, is both ever present and very real.

Unfortunately, risk is hard to estimate and it is often (subconsciously) ignored by investors. After all, most of us would slip into a downward spiral of depression if we spent too much time focusing on the fragility of life and how fortunes, even those built up over many generations, can be lost in a flash. But the reality is that financial markets respond to the broader economic, social, and political environments. They can and do experience both long periods of instability and very sudden and severe corrections.

To invest in markets over a human lifetime, now approaching

a hundred years, seems an impossible task consisting of equal parts prediction and pure speculation. However, while it is impossible to predict with any degree of certainty what financial markets will deliver over the next hundred years, we can review how they have performed over the previous century and look for some important clues.

To help bring this data to life, we turn to a scholarly yet eminently readable book, *Triumph of the Optimists: 101 Years of Global Investment Returns*, in which London Business School professors Elroy Dimson, Paul Marsh, and Mike Staunton provide a carefully reconstructed and detailed picture of global financial market returns from 1900 to 2000.

The twentieth century was, indeed, the "American Century," as *Time* magazine publisher Henry Luce famously declared, as he urged America to enter the Second World War. A dollar invested in the US stock market in 1900 would be worth $862 today, even after accounting for inflation! That statistic speaks for itself. Investing in financial markets is a simple way by which any individual can participate in the economic progress of society and, indeed, those who invested in America were richly rewarded. But viewing that single statistic in isolation is like focusing on the record set by an Olympic gold medalist without an understanding of the sport itself or what it takes to get there. The American experience was far from smooth and must be understood in the appropriate historical and global context.

According to Dimson, Staunton, and Marsh, at the dawn of the twentieth century the five largest world markets by size were the United States, the United Kingdom (without including its vast colonies), Russia, India (at that time the crown jewel of the British Empire), and France. Although the United States was officially at the top of the list, the vast British Empire was really the largest and by far the dominant economic power. The British pound was the reserve currency of the world.

Fast-forward a hundred years to the year 2000, and we find the list consisting of the United States, Japan, the United Kingdom, France, and Germany. China was still emerging as a giant and not yet even on the list.

What is most interesting about this sweep of history is not which countries were added or dropped from the rankings—war, revolution, communism, and the legacy of colonialism offer much in the way of explanation—but rather what happened to financial markets within the countries that managed to maintain or even improve their economic leadership over a hundred-year time span. Consider Great Britain, which started the 1900s in an enviable position, number two, slipping only one spot, to number three, a century later. One might infer that it was an uneventful century for the "vast empire on which the sun never set." It was anything but: in the twentieth century, the British Empire came to an end, the British pound sterling lost its position as the world's reserve currency, and by the 1940s a once-mighty empire was rationing food for its citizens. In the postwar period, Britain would eventually make a successful economic recovery, aligning itself with the United States, but it would never recover its dominant position in the world.

How about the twentieth century's economic winners—the countries that improved their rankings? These nations, too, were anything but oases of stability and prosperity. Japan did not even make the top-ten list of economic powers in 1900 but experienced a meteoric rise and ended the century in the number two slot, even after devastating losses in World War II and the loss of its empire. Meanwhile, France and Germany, both in the top ten in 1900, finished the century each having gained a notch, rising to number four and number five, respectively. Yet both economies were decimated by two world wars that wiped out fortunes. In between the destruction wrought by these conflicts, Germany suffered devastating hyperinflation, which rendered cash savings worthless. In November 1923 in Berlin, a loaf of bread cost 428 billion marks!

The fact is, over the past century, almost every market in the world either has ceased to exist or was shut down for some period of time.

What about the United States? It ranked number one by market capitalization in both 1900 and 2000. With both military and economic dominance, the United States ruled the world stage. The US markets prospered: the Dow Jones Industrial Average, which stood at 55 on December 31, 1899, ended the century at 11,497. The United States delivered "by far the highest uninterrupted real (after inflation) rate of appreciation." Most other countries delivered just a fraction of that.

Still, even in the United States, investing was a dangerous and often gut-wrenching endeavor. The impressive average return of the stock market hides the devastating impact of the Great Depression, two world wars, and even the Vietnam War on so many families. Nor does the average return figure provide any hint of the double-digit inflation of the 1970s and the worrying impact on retirees of that era, or the manic-depressive market that drove the Internet bubble to untenable heights before crashing in the face of reality—and wiping out trillions in wealth. Also well hidden are the changes to the structure of the American economy and demographics, such as the loss of manufacturing jobs, the impact of an aging population, steadily increasing public deficits, and low savings—all factors that caught up with the United States in the great financial crisis of 2008.

Although the United States may well still rank as a dominant economic power at the end of this century, if history is any guide, no one should doubt the arduous road that lies ahead for investors. One way to examine this challenge is to revisit the fate of the companies that dominated the Dow Jones index in 1900. Throughout the twentieth century, Schumpeter's theory of creative destruction—the idea that new innovations create vast wealth, even as they destroy established players—challenged even the most skilled investors. The top US economic sectors in 1900 were railroads, banking, and the building blocks of manufacturing: iron, coal, and steel. By 2000, however, a completely new sector, technology, dominated the economy. Another dominant sector, financials, was about to experience a level of turbulence harking back to the Great Depression.

What was the fate of individual companies? At the turn of the twentieth century, the Dow Jones Industrial Average, created in 1884, was dominated by long-forgotten names such as American Cotton Oil, Distilling & Cattle Feeding, and United States Leather. One of the smaller names in the index, General Electric, was in danger of getting kicked out of this club and indeed would be removed from the index the following year. But GE would return to the Dow Jones index in 1907 and, ironically, it would go on to become the only surviving member of the Dow one hundred years later.

Indeed, by 2000 the Dow was a very different collection of thirty stocks. The largest name on the list, automaker General Motors, delivered an annual profit of $6 billion that year. But the process of creative destruction churned on. In 2009, GM declared bankruptcy, wiping out the stake held by its stockholders. Even so, just one year later, helped by a massive government bailout and stripped of its debilitating debts, the company raised $20.1 billion in what was then the biggest initial public offering in US history.

When markets fail and companies go out of existence, stock market wealth vanishes and equities are transformed into worthless pieces of paper (or, in the modern era, digital detritus). For these reasons, many investors throughout history have instead focused on real estate. Land and property, after all, are tangible, "hard" assets. Perhaps that is why, as the great US bull market of the twentieth century got under way in the wake of the famous 1987 market crash, investors wasted no time diversifying substantial capital into real estate. Which begs the question: What sort of returns can we expect from this asset class over a lifetime?

First, let us acknowledge the unique attributes of real estate. It is one of those rare assets for which governments have created institutions designed to provide loans at below-market prices. In the United States, using a high amount of leverage—for example, making a down payment of 10 to 20 percent to buy a home worth five to ten times that amount—was and is common. In many cases, owners could rent out the property and nearly break even on the carrying costs. This made it possible for speculators to hold property for just a few years before selling it for a tidy profit juiced by debt. Even if the property went up just 10 percent over three years, the seller could make a cool 50 percent on the cash investment because of the five-to-one leverage.

Another factor supporting real estate prices is scarcity. In the early 1990s, certain desirable locales in the United States, such as Palm Beach in Florida, the Upper East Side in Manhattan, and Greenwich, Connecticut, among others, began to see a pickup in the rate of price increases. Single-digit annual increases in value morphed into double-digit annual increases in asking prices. The prevailing theory was that such places were "desirable to both live and invest in," not only for Americans but also for the global elite. After all, the reasoning went, one can't simply duplicate the historic nature of these places, the unique locations, or the exclusive communities that live there. The total supply of land is limited, and our planet is getting more crowded by the minute. Demand outstripped supply, a situation that people thought would never reverse. Not surprisingly, this same exuberance began to inflate real estate prices in less exclusive locations in Arizona, Florida, and Nevada that offered a compelling vision to the aging population: retirement and vacation communities all rolled into one.

One of the first observers to challenge the prevailing wisdom about real estate prices was Yale University economist and Nobel laureate Robert Shiller, who had the foresight (and good fortune!) to publish a book called *Irrational Exuberance* just as the Internet bubble peaked in 2000. In a revised edition of the book published in 2006 (another stroke of masterful timing), Shiller set his analytical sights on property valuations. He argued that no place was so desirable to live that it could sustain double-digit price increases indefinitely. The United States was a large, stable, and rich country, and thus desirable compared to most other places in the world, but it had plenty of raw land. Plus, the real estate boom was not just an American phenomenon: the coast of Spain, the city of London, and all of Ireland were experiencing rocketing real estate prices. The so-called smart money was buying houses and flipping them for double the price—often multiplying their down payments by a factor of five to ten.

To debunk the myth of exclusivity, Shiller turned to the history of real estate prices in desirable European cities like Paris and Amsterdam—cities much like those in the United States, but with earlier starts and much longer histories. Amsterdam, for example, began as a small fishing village in the twelfth century and rose to become a major center for trade in diamonds and for finance. The Dutch would go on to become one of the great seafaring military

powers of the world in the seventeenth century but would eventually lose out to the British in the quest for global trade domination.
Nonetheless, Amsterdam has retained its prominence as a major
hub of European commerce and culture through the ages. Today,
nine hundred years later, the bicycle-friendly city remains a highly
desirable place to live, a home base for some of the world's largest
corporations, and a vibrant mix of culture and fashion that makes
it a major tourist destination in Europe.

If real estate prices anywhere were to deliver skyrocketing returns
over the long haul, surely it would be in Amsterdam. For Professor
Shiller, whose aim was to draw parallels with the then-booming US
real estate market, there were in fact two essential questions: What
was the long-term rate of return of real estate in Amsterdam? And
was the sharply rising US real estate cycle at the time consistent with
the earlier experience of leading European cities?

Since a picture is worth a thousand words, simply glance at the
chart below (Figure 3.1).

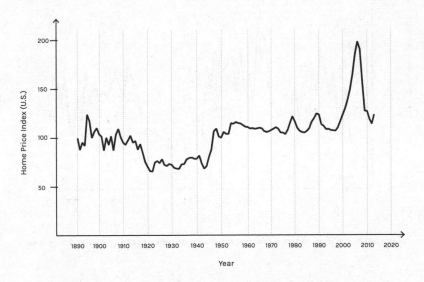

Figure 3.1: One hundred years of real estate prices (USA) (data from the website of
Robert J. Shiller, http://www.econ.yale.edu/~shiller/data.htm)

Drawing upon the work of Professor Shiller, the figure shows a hundred years of property prices in the United States, adjusted for inflation. Clearly, the post-2000 boom in the US market was extraordinary—a fact that would have been abundantly clear to real estate speculators had they bothered to analyze the data.

What about the ritzy neighborhoods of Amsterdam? Were house prices more frothy there, compared to nondescript areas of the city, just like in Manhattan and Palm Beach at the peak of the US market? Researchers can source reliable data, since such storied parts of the city were preserved by the government and the wealthy families who owned property there kept good financial records. Piet Eichholtz, a professor of real estate finance at Maastricht University in the Netherlands, has studied the four-hundred-year history of Amsterdam's prime waterfront district known as Herengracht.

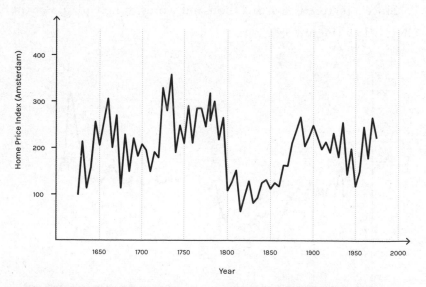

Figure 3.2: The Herengracht Index: four hundred years of real estate prices in Amsterdam

In fact, Professor Eichholtz has created a "Herengracht index" based on detailed sales records of houses in this always fashionable region of the city. Eichholtz's conclusion, as readily apparent in Figure 3.2, was that "from 1628 to 1973 the Herengracht Index doubled in value in real terms."

To put it another way, it would have taken 350 years to double your money—and 250 years just to break even! Over time, undeveloped land, the rise of other cities, and shifting political and economic sands all have a way of getting overvalued real estate assets back to their true value.

So if countries and markets can experience long periods of instability or very severe corrections, and if markets like real estate simply don't rise in the way that people expect, what is an investor to do? Survival clearly requires diversification and staying power. Markets usually do correct through the process of mean reversion, but one cannot know how long that will take, and the process can destroy fortunes. That offers very little comfort to individual investors. The takeaway is this: markets alone cannot provide you with an adequate financial safety net. Therefore, *markets alone cannot and should not be the only solution for managing your wealth.* In fact, the next chapter is devoted to illuminating a particularly dangerous aspect of financial markets.

Speculative Bubbles and Market Manias

Figure 4.1: *Weiji*

The mandarin word for crisis, *weiji*, is often said to be composed of two characters, one representing danger (*wei*, as in *weixian* 危险) and the other opportunity (*ji*, as in *jihui* 机会). But according to Nicola Di Cosmo, Luce Foundation Professor in East Asian Studies at the Institute for Advanced Study, this turns out to be a linguistic urban legend. *Weiji* does indeed mean "crisis," but the formulation is instead a combination of the words *danger* and *moment* or *inflection point*. In the Chinese language, therefore, a crisis can be interpreted as a sudden turn for the worse in an already perilous situation, not as a fork in the road between danger and opportunity. Possibly, it implies the imperative to act swiftly as a perilous situation escalates and worsens.

When it comes to investing, the bewildering yet intoxicating confusion of danger with opportunity can fuel one of the most treacherous market events that you will encounter in your financial life: major speculative bubbles, which have existed as long as markets themselves and recur with startling frequency.

As in the aftermath of a rioting mob, speculative bubbles leave a trail of destruction, many financially wounded investors (some fatally, alas), and lots of questions in desperate need of answers: How did the bubble start? What gave it momentum? When was the inflection point? Why didn't we stop it? Why did I participate? Why didn't I get out of the market while I could have? How could I have been so stupid? Could it happen again?

The complex interplay of social, economic, and psychological elements that creates speculative bubbles is often underappreciated. So are the signs, usually imperceptible at first, that the mood is shifting and the bubble is about to burst. *Sky and Water*, the famous wood print by Dutch artist M. C. Escher (Figure 4.2), nicely illustrates this type of gradual shift.

Figure 4.2: M. C. Escher, *Sky and Water I*, wood print, 1938 (M. C. Escher's *Sky and Water I*, copyright © 2014, the M. C. Escher Company, the Netherlands. All rights reserved. www.mcescher.com)

As your eye scans it from top to bottom, the picture seamlessly transforms from a flock of birds in the sky into a school of fish in the sea, much as the news headlines can turn a raging bull market into a bear market. Such complexities make bubbles exceedingly difficult (if not impossible) to recognize during their formative stage, even harder to avoid as they gather strength, and often simply too dangerous to fight at their peak. Nonetheless, in order for you to enjoy stability in your financial life, you must learn to navigate and withstand the instability that speculative manias force upon the entire market.

The archetype of markets gone mad remains, even today, the Dutch tulip bubble of the 1630s. In the first serious analysis of this event, Scottish journalist Charles Mackay captured the essence of the speculative frenzy in his 1841 book, *Extraordinary Popular Delusions and the Madness of Crowds*: "Many individuals grew suddenly rich. A golden bait hung temptingly out before the people, and one after another, they rushed to the tulip marts, like flies around a honey-pot. . . . At last, however, the more prudent began to see that this folly could not last forever. Rich people no longer bought the flowers to keep them in their gardens, but to sell them again at cent for cent profit. It was seen that somebody must lose fearfully in the end. As this conviction spread, prices fell, and never rose again."

What might have been the transformational change that the Dutch thought tulip bulbs would bring? Although it remains somewhat of a mystery, a variety of explanations have been put forth. Historians have postulated that the bubonic plague—which preceded the tulip mania and wiped out a seventh of the population—had created a heightened societal desire to enjoy the finer things in life while one could. While the role of the bubonic plague in creating the tulip bubble may be speculative at best, there is general agreement that a watershed event in the bursting of the tulip bubble began when no one turned up at a tulip auction in the Dutch town of Haarlem. The town was in the middle of a plague outbreak. Apparently the flowers were not to die for.

Social scientists have explored the context for the bubble. In the seventeenth century, a time of unprecedented wealth for many in Dutch society, owning and cultivating rare tulips was a sign of culture. It brought entrée into high society, much like acquiring rare pieces of art does today. Monetary economists have also weighed in: they point out that Amsterdam, which was already among the wealthiest cities in Europe, was experiencing a sharp rise in the money supply, thanks to the spoils of theft and war. It is not surprising that some of this money would be available to fan the flames of speculation. Interestingly, economists in the efficient markets camp have put forward an alternative thesis. They argue that the economic folly of investing in rare tulips was not readily apparent at the time. The ability to plant the flowers and sell them to future generations, even for a fraction of the original cost, provided at least the illusion of downside protection.

These economists also correctly point out that tulip bulb "investments" were completely disconnected from reality, not only in terms of the economic fundamentals but also in terms of actual transactions. This occurred because of a financial innovation in the Dutch market. In 1637 the Dutch created a financial instrument called tulip futures. While the futures market facilitated trades between farmers and buyers without the exchange of large amounts of coin, it also fueled a speculative market that got out of control. At the height of the bubble, most purchases were based on credit and took the form of contracts in the tulip futures markets.

Speculators were simply buying what they could not afford and selling what they did not own. Indeed, Dutch courts that dealt with the aftermath of the tulip bubble regarded most outstanding agreements as a form of gambling and simply invalidated them. Those contracts that were not nullified were often unenforceable.

While fragile tulips trading at ridiculous prices is an easy image to conjure up while describing the insanity of bubbles, it misses a crucial point. Manias do not grow and sustain themselves unless there is an underlying, easily understandable value proposition: the breakthrough that attracted investor capital in the first place. In fact, speculative bubbles are often preceded by a period of technological innovation that creates wealth for society but that also produces, as economist Joseph Schumpeter has observed, economic and social dislocations that upend the existing order. Some scholars contend that bubbles develop not just because of investors' animal spirits but rather because of the speculative uncertainty about future productivity that exists in the midst of a technological revolution (and that can be recognized as folly only after the fact). This much is clear: for investors to participate in a bubble, they must believe that the investment in question is a "once-in-a-lifetime opportunity." For this reason, one feature that is common to all bubbles is an underlying investment theme that investors can understand and readily communicate—one that, at least for a time, they fervently believe to be self-evident.

A number of other famous market manias have tripped up investors through the ages. In the 1700s, the famous South Sea bubble, which sucked in among its many famous victims the physicist Isaac Newton, grew out of enthusiasm for the increased competition between European powers to control the sea trade. In the 1840s, the "transformative power of the iron horse" led to the even bigger but less well-known British Railway bubble, which repeated in the United States at the tail end of the nineteenth century, afflicting US railway stocks from 1873 to 1894. The "roaring" 1920s were driven, in no small measure, by the euphoria from the end of the First World War and a desire by the general public to acquire the new wonders of the manufacturing world such as cars and radios, most of it on credit. This, of course, ended badly in 1929 and led to the Great Depression.

More recently, from 1998 to 2000, the Internet and telecom stock bubble resulted in a massive run-up and collapse of the NASDAQ stock market (see Figures 4.3 and 4.4), fueled by forecasts of infinite demand for bandwidth and an almost manic belief that new economy stocks would forever change the dynamics of traditional commerce. In the United States alone, network infrastructure companies spent $30 billion to build 90 million miles of fiber-optic cable. These massive investments were a decade too early. The same glut of fiber-optic cable in the first Internet revolution laid the foundations of Web 2.0, or the networked economy.

Today when we look at the current valuations of several social networking ventures, the word *bubble* is ever present in one's mind. As the networking economy comes into its own, one can depend on the infectious optimism of entrepreneurs, the well-oiled machines of Silicon Valley and Wall Street, and hungry investors with dollar signs in their eyes to create a new set of sky-high valuations. Which of these companies will pan out to become the next Google, Amazon, or Facebook, and which of these will become the next great idea with bad execution or just bad luck, remains the multibillion-dollar question.

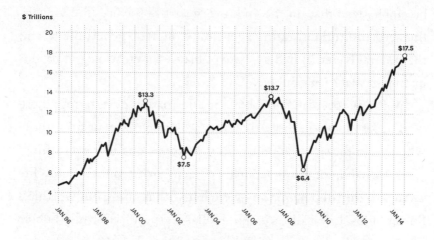

Figure 4.3: S&P market capitalization

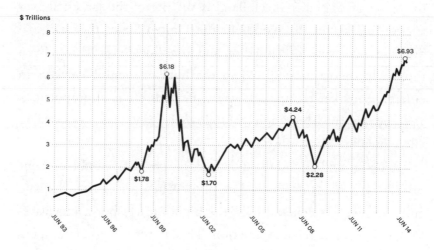

Figure 4.4: NASDAQ market capitalization

The US housing bubble, which burst in 2008 and quickly morphed into a global financial crisis, had at its origin an even more fundamentally American value proposition: that owning a house was one of the best investments a family could make. It must be emphasized that, in the end, every part of society (individuals, financial institutions, rating agencies, Congress, government, and the Federal Reserve) had its share of blame for creating and participating in that mega-bubble.

With any speculative bubble, the aftermath is devastating: those who make money in the early stages are often different from those who join in the speculation late in the game—and lose everything.

In Holland, for example, many citizens forfeited their entire life savings to the tulip mania and were left with nothing but worthless flower bulbs. Ironically, though, Holland's speculative tulip bubble did leave at least one positive legacy: to this day, the country remains the center of production for the European floral market, and the town of Aalsmeer in Holland is the site of the largest flower auction market in the world. In the United States the marginal home owners were foreclosed on and lost almost everything. Even those who never participated in the bubble, such as workers in emerging market economies, were affected, often disproportionately, by the global recession that followed. Why, then, does society allow such bubbles to form?

To better understand the dynamics of speculative bubbles, consider how markets normally function. When prices rise, demand falls. But even as demand falls, the higher prices boost incentives for suppliers to increase production. This, in turn, further dampens the prospect of future price increases and leads to a new market equilibrium price. The reverse is also true: a drop in price boosts demand but reduces production incentives, dampening the prospect of future price decreases. In a bubble, however, increases in price actually *increase demand* because investors are convinced—for either legitimate or fraudulent reasons—that the price increases signal rising demand and ever-higher prices into the future. The connection between price and value (utility) is broken and replaced by speculation. Rather than stabilizing market fluctuations, increasing prices fuel speculation that ultimately feeds on itself.

Many different economic factors can drive speculative bubbles. Shortages of a key component used in the manufacture of an expensive product, such as an airplane, might incentivize manufacturers to pay a much higher price than the component is intrinsically worth, so as not to disrupt the entire delivery pipeline. The result is a spike in the price until new suppliers enter the market. This explains why regulators seek to prevent monopolies from forming.

Commodities markets are also prone to speculative booms and busts, but for a different reason: mines, steel plants, and aluminum smelters take a fair amount of time and money to start up and maintain. During a glut, these massive operations begin to lose substantial amounts of money and at some point are closed down. When demand picks up again, however, they cannot be instantly brought back into production. In fact, given the substantial cost, owners may wait to ensure that demand is robust enough to justify start-up investment. Thus achieving equilibrium between supply and demand may take months or even years.

Regardless of the underlying economics, speculative bubbles are rooted in human psychology. They are a manifestation of what economist John Maynard Keynes called "animal spirits": our propensity to make decisions based on a "spontaneous urge to action," in Keynes's words, rather than on a careful consideration of weighted probabilities, as rational economic theory would suggest.

Consider how behavioral traps come together to fuel a mania.

In an initial phase, investors make mistakes in forecasting demand for the underlying technology or innovation by simply *extrapolating* the current situation (rising demand) into the future rather than thinking about how markets and people actually adjust to increasing prices. As increasing numbers of investors participate in the mania, everyone derives a false sense of confidence. It must be OK if everyone is doing it! This is often accompanied by a fear of being left behind. Indeed, while the bubble is inflating, such *herd behavior* protects those who move with the crowd and often punishes those who don't. As the famous Keynesian economist John Kenneth Galbraith put it, somewhat tartly: "The euphoric episode is protected and sustained by the will of those who are involved, in order to justify the circumstances that are making them rich. And it is equally protected by the will to ignore, exorcise, or condemn those who express doubts."

When the bubble reaches unsustainable proportions, things get out of control, competition for spoils becomes fiercer, and legitimate business transactions beget fraud and corruption. Indeed, with big profits at stake, the boundary between ethical and unethical behavior gets fuzzy. The underlying driver in this phase of a mania is *moral hazard*: a situation where a select few individuals earn most of the return, while leaving someone else to shoulder the risk. In a typical situation involving moral hazard, the players enjoying the spoils often know who the sucker is—and they know (or at least firmly believe) it's not them.

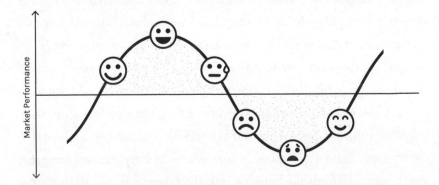

Figure 4.5: Investor emotions during different stages of a market cycle

Finally, at the height of a mania, the intrinsic value of the asset that triggered the frenzy is no longer of consequence. Instead, the bubble sustains itself thanks to *the greater fools syndrome*, a scenario in which buyers (the fools) purchase assets at increasingly absurd prices, convinced that they will be able to sell them later to others (the greater fools) at a tidy profit. The greater fools syndrome is related to a behavioral bias known as *illusory superiority*, which describes investors' mistaken belief that they are smarter than the average investor and will be able to cash out before the bubble bursts. The attentive reader will recognize that the same bias was previously discussed in the context of the overconfidence observed when the average car driver evaluated his or her own driving skills in relation to others.

Perhaps the most maddening aspect of bubbles is the fact that they provide opportunities to create wealth at a scale that simply cannot be achieved by investing in an unleveraged, diversified portfolio in a normal market environment. Burgeoning bubbles that are based on genuine technological breakthroughs *can in fact sow the seeds for upward wealth mobility*, as the tech bubble did for the founders and early investors in companies like Google and Amazon.

Not only do people participating early in the bubble often become much wealthier, but also those who opt out become relatively poorer. A technological bubble may lead to a change in valuations for many parts of the economy, which means that those not partaking in the feast may see their purchasing power and net worth diminish.

Your future depends on balancing risk and reward throughout your life's journey and maximizing the probability that you will achieve your most important goals. Substantial wealth creation is itself a reasonable goal and not one to be overlooked. At a societal level, in fact, it is critical for attracting capital in support of the new ideas and technologies that power economies. But to be successful in the pursuit of high-return opportunities that yield great wealth, you must frame your goals and constrain the potential risk so that you aren't pursuing your aspirations at the expense of your overall financial security. Thankfully, with the right framework in place to guide your decisions, you shouldn't have to choose. With a disciplined process around risk allocation in place, you can improve your odds of participating in the wealth-creating potential of innovation and entrepreneurship while at the same time lowering the risk of succumbing to the wealth-destroying bubbles and manias that have afflicted investors for centuries.

WEALTH

How Do People Become (Very) Wealthy?

Every year, the US government collects vast amounts of data on the net worth of families across the country. Number crunchers at the Federal Reserve, the nation's central bank, analyze Americans' net income, credit card debt, the value of homes and mortgages, bank balances, investment portfolios, and more. These data are cleaned up, dissected, tabulated, and published every three years as *The Federal Reserve Survey of Consumer Finances*. Notwithstanding its dry name, the report provides a fascinating yet sobering portrait of the wealth distribution in what is arguably one of the wealthiest countries on the planet.

As students of the hard and soft sciences well know, the typical spread of randomly distributed data often resembles a bell curve, whether it's the variation in performance on a standardized test or the height or weight of children in a fourth-grade class. Most data points cluster toward the average, creating a pronounced hump in the center of the curve, with fewer data points extending symmetrically outward on both sides. This distribution is so common that statisticians refer to it as the "normal distribution."

The wealth distribution in America stands in sharp contrast.

When the household net worth of all US families is mapped onto a graph, as shown in figure 5.1, the resulting picture reveals a very skewed distribution of wealth.

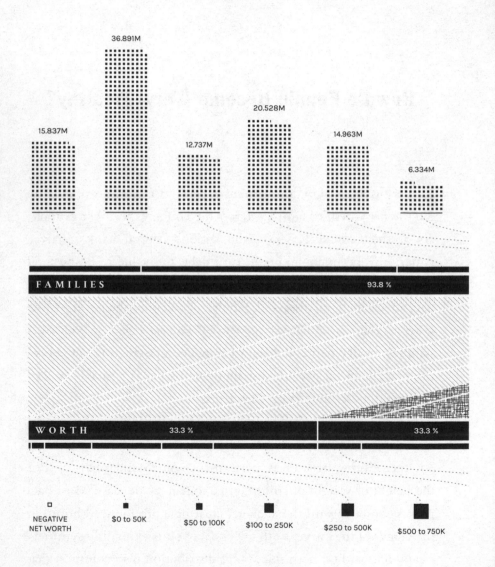

Figure 5.1: The wealth spectrum of America

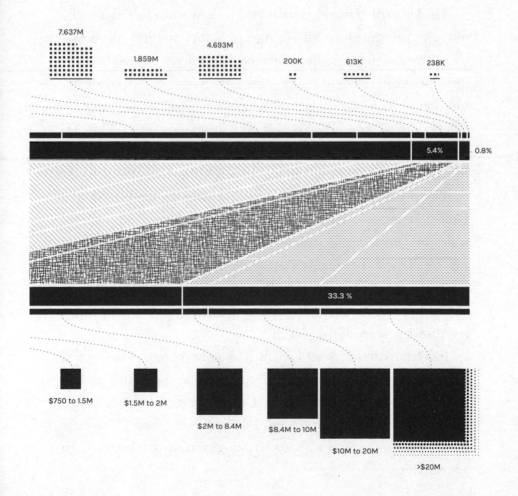

• = 100,000 FAMILIES

7.637M

1.859M

4.693M

200K

613K

238K

5.4%

0.8%

33.3 %

$750 to 1.5M

$1.5M to 2M

$2M to 8.4M

$8.4M to 10M

$10M to 20M

>$20M

As "The Wealth Spectrum of America" demonstrates, wealth is neither uniformly nor normally distributed. Instead, there is a "long tail," implying a concentration of wealth among a few. In fact, a third of the nation's wealth is shared by the bottom 93 percent of all families—those with a net worth below $1.5 million. A second third is shared by the roughly 6 percent of Americans who possess between $1.5 million and $7 million in net worth. The final third is controlled by just 1 percent of the population with upwards of $7 million, a group that includes the members of the elite Forbes 400, the business magazine's famous annual ranking of US billionaires.

The long tail of wealth distribution by household is in fact nothing new: throughout the Middle Ages in Europe and Asia, the nobility and landowning families maintained a firm grip on resources in their nations and enjoyed a gilded life, even as most of the population toiled in poverty. The Industrial Revolution brought vast improvements in living standards as power from steam, coal, and oil supplemented human labor, and democracy and property rights took hold in Western societies, lifting millions of people into the middle classes.

The distribution of wealth, while markedly uneven in the United States, is even more skewed when analyzed on a global scale. For instance, according to a recent report that carefully sources the world's roughly $241 trillion in total wealth, the richest 1 percent of adults control 46 percent of global assets and the richest 10 percent control 86 percent. The bottom 50 percent hold less than 1 percent of the wealth.

Indeed, recent work by French economist Thomas Piketty and collaborators points to wealth inequality as an inevitable consequence of the capitalistic system. This has in turn led to a robust debate over capitalism's unintended consequences, such as inequality of opportunity, and what society or governments should do to address this.

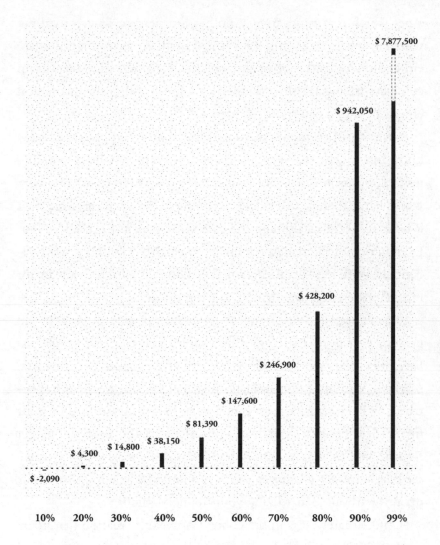

Figure 5.2: US wealth spectrum in percentiles (source: 2013 Survey of Consumer Finances)

With roughly 20 percent of the world's population living on less than a dollar a day, one takeaway from our snapshot of wealth distribution is that Americans are comparatively lucky. Yet the reality is that most Americans' financial situation is quite precarious. As shown in Figure 5.2, which presents the US wealth spectrum by percentiles, one out of ten US households is bankrupt, possessing a net worth that is negative. Another ten percent have a total net worth of less than $4,300. One-third of all American families are either already bankrupt or just one cataclysmic event away from complete financial ruin, whether it's a job layoff, a major medical emergency, or a bad traffic accident.

Such statistics reinforce something that most people already know intuitively: that even in America, a country whose founding mythology promises a shot at success and fortune to anyone who works hard, there is still a deep asymmetry between the sweat that it takes to build wealth and the ease with which it can all be lost. Even in one of the richest countries on earth—a country, not incidentally, with few social safety nets—money is hard to come by for most families, and even harder to hang on to.

The central lessons are clear: whatever degree of wealth you possess, you need a strategy that enables you to *preserve what you have*, regardless of the performance of the economy or financial markets. You must also *maintain your standing* on the wealth spectrum, by keeping pace with inflation and earning a return on your financial assets that is at least equivalent to the broader market return. And finally, if your aspirations include *moving up the wealth spectrum or creating a lasting impact*, you should be able to pursue your dreams without jeopardizing your financial safety.

Unfortunately, it is in the context of wealth creation that many investors falter. That's because the allure of creating substantial wealth leads even those with the best of intentions down a path of highly questionable investment decisions. For example, investors often become excessively aggressive during bull markets only to reverse course after suffering extreme losses when the market turns, or they take on a large mortgage without having adequate safety reserves in place to mitigate a potential job loss during an economic recession.

At the same time, though, the reality is that many people *do* create vast fortunes. According to the Cap Gemini World Wealth 2013 report, there are about 12 million high-net-worth individuals worldwide, defined as those owning at least $1 million in assets not counting their primary residence and associated artifacts. Interestingly, at the very high end of the wealth distribution, one finds a similar long-tailed distribution as described earlier.

So what lessons can be gleaned for those who desire upward wealth mobility?

One of the best ways to answer this question is to analyze how the ultra-wealthy earned their money, based on what is arguably the most definitive guide available to the story of wealth in America: the Forbes 400 list. Just as the Academy Awards and the Grammys create buzz and excitement well beyond the entertainment and music industries, the business magazine's famous ranking captivates the business world and the general public alike. Its enduring popularity is a mark of the fascination and admiration with which everyday Americans view the creators and beneficiaries of great fortunes. And great they are: according to the 2014 list, the average net worth of the four hundred richest Americans was $5.7 billion. The net worth required to make the list? $1.55 billion. A total of 113 billionaires could not make the list!

From its start, the Forbes 400 has focused the spotlight on an astonishing level of wealth creation—and concentration. In 1982, its inaugural year, the combined net worth of the list was equivalent to 2.8 percent of US gross domestic product, and a minimum net worth of just under $100 million was required to make the list, which contained just thirteen billionaires. By 2006 the list had become the exclusive domain of billionaires and accounted for as much as 9.5 percent of US GDP. As Peter Bernstein and Annalyn Swan note in their book about the list, *All the Money in the World,* only the Gilded Age and the Roaring Twenties "can withstand comparison to the last 25 years in terms of wealth accumulation." After a dip in fortunes during the global financial crisis, the fortunes of America's most wealthy have again accelerated: according to *Forbes*, by 2013 the wealthiest as a group had gained back all they had lost in the crisis, and their combined net worth of more than $2 trillion was roughly equal to the gross domestic product of Russia. By 2014, Russia's fortune appeared to be in decline, but not so that of the Forbes 400. They now had a combined net worth of $2.29 trillion, roughly equal to the gross domestic product of Brazil.

Not all of the billionaires on the Forbes 400 are self-made. Studies point to an almost equal mix of people who began with nothing, others who grew up in comfortable circumstances, and others still who inherited either a little wealth or considerable assets. That's only democratic, after all: the fact that your family had a bit of money and that you didn't have to sell newspapers as a kid to make ends meet should not prevent you from making it onto the Forbes 400. Perhaps the broadest generalization we can make about the list is that, regardless of how much money these individuals started with, most have succeeded brilliantly at transforming some level of initial capital into far greater fortunes.

Interestingly, the sources of wealth for the Forbes 400 fall neatly into just four categories: business owners, financiers, inheritors, and real estate veterans. The majority of those on the list, 60 percent, fall into the first category. They had a vision, launched a business or brand name, and put their heart and soul into it. Actually, they poured everything they owned into the idea. As the business flourished, they didn't pull out but rather reinvested the proceeds, borrowed even more money when necessary, and built the company into a lasting enterprise. Along the way there were innumerable risks, lawsuits, economic downturns, and other challenges.

What we see reflected in the Forbes 400 are the survivors: the Bill Gateses and Oprah Winfreys of the world. Of course, it is hard to think of Bill Gates and Oprah Winfrey as "survivors," so a better term would be "winners"—those who prevailed in a long, risky, and often brutal struggle, who relentlessly and successfully monetized their talent (human capital) and expanded while mitigating risk at every stage.

In an earlier chapter we bemoaned the investment performance of the average active money manager. But what about those managers who perform well above average? It turns out that they represent 20 percent of the Forbes 400. In addition to Warren Buffett, these names include the most successful hedge fund and private equity managers, such as global macro investor George Soros and David Bonderman, a cofounder of private equity firm Texas Pacific Group, whose portfolio companies employ more than six hundred thousand people and have included everything from fast-food chain Burger King to Continental Airlines. Other names in this category, such as Bill Gross (cofounder and former CIO of the giant bond manager PIMCO) and Edward Johnson III and daughter Abigail (Fidelity Investments), have built up giant financial service companies by delivering superior performance and service.

Also of note on this exclusive list is a personal favorite, James H. Simons, my investment mentor and chair of the investment committee at the Institute for Advanced Study, where I was the chief investment officer for several years. Jim is a Renaissance man with three successful pursuits: mathematics, finance, and philanthropy. A distinguished mathematician in his own right, he went on to found the most successful hedge fund ever and is now in the process of giving away most of his money to scientific research and education. In 2006, the *Financial Times* described him simply as "the world's smartest billionaire."

Inheritance and marriage is everyone's favorite Forbes 400 category and accounts for 12 percent of the fortunes on the list. Earning wealth this way is, shall we say, highly risky and idiosyncratic. It is not, however, a very large category, confirming the impression that in America most wealth is self-made. This does not mean that those listed in other categories did not inherit a business or a sizable amount of wealth from their parents. But it does mean that the men and women in the other three categories took what they got to an entirely new level. To be fair, many of the occupants of this category remain actively involved in the family business or in charitable activities of the family foundation.

Finally, we turn to real estate, which accounts for 8 percent of Forbes 400 wealth. Land and property investments have played a major role in wealth creation in every society. Even those members of the Forbes 400 who did not get wealthy primarily through real estate investing often have significant holdings of this asset class. What distinguishes the individuals who make the list, such as New York's Donald Trump or Chicago developer Sam Zell, is that they are intimately familiar with the vicious boom and bust cycles of real estate and excel at managing cash flows and complex construction projects alike, while often making extensive use of borrowed money (non-recourse leverage, to be exact).

Our rough categorization of the Forbes 400 may be considered somewhat arbitrary. We could have rolled the money management and real estate categories into the business category. Alternatively, we could have carved out new categories according to business sectors represented on the list, such as software or retail. But that would not change the answer to a central question: *What do the investment strategies that yield great wealth have in common?*

The answer is simple. At least initially, all of these paths to great fortunes were idiosyncratic strategies that involved monetizing their brain power, knowledge, and expertise (that is, their own human capital and that of their employees) through the use of two potentially perilous elements: leverage and concentration (along with hard work and lots of luck, of course). Concentration and leverage may have also been present in a non-economic sense: for example, individuals on the list may have been able to leverage family access to political capital or derived a connection or benefit by virtue of belonging to a particular professional or social network.

The point is that the super-rich did not earn their wealth by building conventional portfolios based on the principles of asset allocation and diversification. In fact, they did just the opposite. All four primary sources of wealth creation represented in the Forbes 400 involve "idiosyncratic risk"—the kind of risk that, according to the tenets of modern portfolio theory, "rational" investors can and should eliminate by diversification. Yet most of the people on the list believed, and still believe, that focusing on what they know best is the least risky strategy.

Imitating the investment strategies of the Forbes 400 is not for the faint of heart. Nor is it necessarily sensible. Think of it this way: buying a lottery ticket after watching a television interview with a newly minted Powerball multimillionaire won't improve your chances of winning. Making decisions based on success stories, while ignoring failures, is a common behavioral pitfall known as "survivor bias" and often leads to missteps and disappointment.

Which brings us to another important point: *the strategies for making wealth and keeping wealth are not necessarily one and the same.* The struggle to keep a balance between creating and preserving wealth is a non-trivial one. In fact, one of the most remarkable aspects of the Forbes 400 is its incredible volatility, in terms of both the enormous swings in wealth among those on the list and the fluidity with which people come and go from the list.

The 2014 Forbes 400 ranking revealed that thirty-six billion-aires were poorer than the previous year, and twenty-six people had dropped off the list.

In fact, according to one analysis, only thirty-six individuals who made the original list in 1982 stayed rich enough, and stayed alive long enough, to qualify for the Forbes 400 for the next twenty-four consecutive years. Back then, 13 percent of the list came from just three families: eleven Hunts, fourteen Rockefellers, and twenty-eight du Ponts. By 2002, these three families were down to just one, three, and zero members, respectively. Fast-forward to 2010: Ray Lee Hunt, with $3.2 billion, ranked 62 and was the sole Hunt family member. David Rockefeller, with $2.4 billion, was ranked 132 and was the only Rockefeller. The lone reference to the du Ponts was an unfortunate one: a mere mention of John E. du Pont, who made the list from 1982 to 1987 and was dying while serving a life sentence for murder.

One of the most interesting studies of churn on the Forbes 400 was conducted in 2004 by my longtime colleague and research collaborator, Lex Zaharoff. This research was based on an extensive analysis of the reasons why people dropped off of the Forbes 400. Consistent with the findings in Bernstein and Swan's *All the Money in the World*, Zaharoff and his team found that just 15 percent of the names, a mere fifty-four individuals, stayed on the list every year from 1982 to 2003. Of the 346 names that were no longer on the list, the researchers determined that 141 individuals, or 36 percent, had dropped off due to non-risk reasons, such as the recalculation or reclassification of their wealth by *Forbes* or death and distribution of wealth to family members, foundations, and the taxman. Of the remaining 205 dropouts, a majority, 59 percent, fell off the list because the wealth did not grow fast enough or there was an outright erosion of the wealth.

Zaharoff and his colleagues then analyzed the cause of each exit from the list and identified a combination of eight risk factors that played a role in each case. They are as follows:

- Concentration
- Leverage
- Excessive spending
- Taxes
- Family dynamics
- Liability
- Currency
- Government action

Interestingly, the first two factors on this list, the double-edged swords of concentration and leverage, are precisely the factors we identified earlier as the keys to earning your way into the Forbes 400. The rest of these factors are simply additional risks that, for these individuals, could not or were not effectively mitigated and eventually caused the individual to lose excessive wealth relative to peers on the list. Zaharoff concludes his report with a recommendation: that as individuals and families move from wealth creation to wealth preservation, they must shift the types of risks that they take.

Staying "wealthiest" isn't possible without taking risk, however. According to Zaharoff's research, if all the wealth in the Forbes 400 had been allocated to US Treasury bills in 1982, for example, every individual would have fallen off the list by 2003, based on the rate of return on US government debt. *Thus to both preserve assets and grow wealth, it is imperative to shift from strategies built on concentration and leverage to a diversified portfolio of risks.* The secret is finding the right balance among safety, growth, and investments with the potential to create significant wealth—and that may or may not involve leverage and concentration.

You must begin this process by figuring out what you require to meet your essential needs and to reach your *aspirational goals*.

For the Forbes 400 $1 billion is just not enough to get onto the list. What is your number?

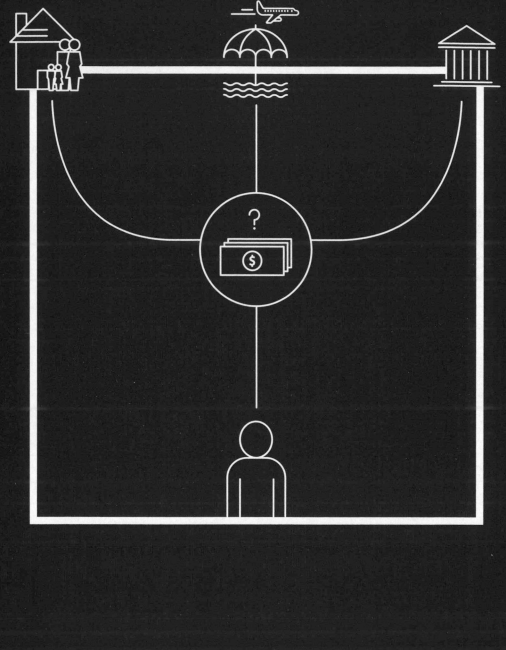

How Much (Money) Do I Need?

*A*m I on track? It's a deceptively simple, four-word question that bedevils every investor, regardless of wealth. In the context of retirement planning, this question tends to be especially vexing. That's because most people make two mistakes when thinking about retirement: they usually *overestimate* how much money they need to be happy, and they usually *underestimate* how much money they will need in order to sustain their current standard of living in the future.

Experts disagree on exactly how many Americans are financially well equipped for retirement, but the research is alarming. According to the Employee Benefit Research Institute, only 18 percent of working Americans say they are very confident about having enough money to retire comfortably—and more than half have saved less than $25,000. The lack of preparedness is not new. In a study conducted prior to the 2008 financial crisis, Boston College's well-regarded Center for Retirement Research found that 43 percent of US households were "at risk" of being unable to maintain their preretirement standard of living in retirement.

The reality is that most people do not save enough money. It's a question of simple mathematics. Let's assume that starting from age twenty onward you will earn money for forty-five years, retire at age sixty-five, and live to be ninety. In other words, you will save for forty-five years and spend what you saved for the next twenty-five years. The percentage of income that you must save annually to avoid outliving your money can be expressed as follows:

REQUIRED PERCENTAGE OF AFTER-TAX INCOME TO BE SAVED

=

(# OF RETIREMENT YEARS)

_____

(# OF WORKING + RETIREMENT YEARS)

Thus in our hypothetical example, the amount of money that would need to be saved—money that would build net worth, including investing in a home, funding social security, and so on—is roughly 35 percent of your after-tax income.

25/(45+25) = 25/70 = 35%

There are some caveats with this rough but simple calculation. For example, your required savings rate would be reduced by any pension or Social Security benefits. But the point is that this back-of-the envelope calculation suggests a baseline savings rate of 35 percent—one that is many times higher than the average US household savings rate of just 3 to 5 percent.

Rather than following a disciplined retirement savings strategy, many people rely on their gut and make intuitive estimates of a single, aspirational number that reflects the amount of money they think they need in the bank to enjoy retirement bliss. This is often referred to as "the Number"—the minimum required net worth that would enable you to say to the world: *"That's it. I'm done!"*

So what's your Number? Think about it for a minute. Was it always the same—or has it changed over the years? Or is there no number that would move you to retire because you always want to be working in one capacity or another?

It turns out that the more money you are worth today, the more you probably feel you need to accumulate further before calling it quits. Consider the goal of becoming a millionaire, a popular and still attainable goal for Americans living at the median US wealth level of $125,000 and who still have plenty of working years ahead of them. When upwardly mobile middle-class Americans move into the ranks of millionaires, rather than celebrating, many are more likely to focus on the fact that $1 million is not what it used to be and may not be nearly enough to sustain their lifestyle in retirement. Indeed, in the United States alone there are roughly 3 million millionaires these days, so they are not exactly a rarity.

Once these Americans accumulate a net worth of $2 million to $3 million, they begin to enjoy some sense of financial security and success—but soon realize that $5 million is the true inflection point between merely affluent and wealthy. Those with $5 million want $10 million. Those with $10 million think $25 million or even $50 million would do the trick. And so it goes all the way up to the Forbes 400, where $1 billion is simply the cover charge. The irony is that, along the way, everyone who is not in financial distress recognizes full well—or claims to recognize—that they are not in it for the money.

Lee Eisenberg, a former editor of *Esquire* magazine, captured this constant resetting of expectations in a provocative 2006 book called *The Number.* The inspiration for Eisenberg's book, which, appropriately enough, featured a nest egg on its cover, was the author's own struggle to understand exactly how much money he needed to sustain himself and his wife in retirement. The process of answering this seemingly simple numerical question led him to much deeper questions about what kind of life he wanted to lead, in the present and in the future.

Eisenberg captured many interesting aspects of how people think about money and how interconnected money has become with almost every aspect of our lives. Most interesting and telling of all, perhaps, is his conversation with an anonymous Wall Street type whom Eisenberg calls "Deep Pockets." When Eisenberg asks him to explain how he thinks the Number "works its will" among the relatively well-off people he knows, Deep Pockets describes four types of lifestyles: "Comfortable, Comfortable Plus, Kind of Rich, and Rich."

The archetypes, according to "Deep Pockets" are:

- Comfortable: lives in one place, eats/travels modestly, though better than most, then you need $50,000 to $100,000 a year, which means a number from $1 million to $2 million.
- Comfortable +: country club, second home . . . then you need $175,000 to $200,000 a year or a number ranging from $2 million to $5 million.
- Kind of Rich: couple of houses, gives away money, likes the finer things of life . . . then you need $350,000 to $500,000 or a number of about $7 million to $10 million.
- Rich+: a place for every season, fractional jet shares for travel, sits on boards . . . then you need $1 million plus a year and a number greater than $20 million.

Eisenberg does not describe the underlying assumptions behind Deep Pockets's rough calculation, though the number specified is about twenty times the expected annual spending. Indeed, almost every financial firm has a detailed retirement calculator that will provide you with an estimate of what you need to retire. The problem is that to arrive at your Number, either they or you must quantify several key inputs that in most cases are simply educated guesses. Some are estimates of your life expectancy, current income, and anticipated retirement age, as well as future inflation, tax rates, and stock returns. Based on the assumptions used by the calculator, and by adjusting the variables, notably the estimated rate of return of your portfolio, you can, frankly, arrive at almost any Number.

The sheer uncertainty of future equity market performance is an especially intractable problem in determining your Number. As we have discussed, the recurrence of financial crises and the turbulent history of markets suggest that stock returns are not exactly dependable. Equities should and historically have delivered positive real return, when averaged over long periods of time. But in the long run, as economist John Maynard Keynes famously said, we're all dead. If your standard of living is dependent on the future performance of the stock market, then you must be able to absorb extreme losses and survive the stretches of time when there are no returns at all.

What you really need is a framework to achieve your *essential goals* no matter what the market does: one that at least minimizes the impact of year-to-year market fluctuations on your probability of success. Using such a framework, the key to providing a satisfying answer to the question "Am I on track?" rests not on the unpredictability of financial markets but rather on how effectively you identify, prioritize, and quantify your goals and adapt your investment strategy appropriately along the way.

Your goals and aspirations seem so personal, and perhaps so

idiosyncratic, that they may defy any attempt to create a general framework that would logically organize them, let alone build a wealth management strategy to achieve them. But the work of one of the stars of academic psychology, Abraham Maslow, helps point the way.

In the early 1950s, Maslow was pioneering a new approach to the study of human behavior. Instead of focusing on the mentally ill, as was the convention at the time, he studied "exemplary people"—the top 1 percent of achievers in various fields, such as contemporaries Albert Einstein and Eleanor Roosevelt. Maslow's groundbreaking work, the basis of what is today called humanistic psychology, includes a breakdown of the psychological underpinnings of human aspirations. These are often illustrated in a famous pyramid known as *Maslow's hierarchy of needs* (Figure 6.1).

SELF-ACTUALIZATION
Personal growth, fulfillment

SELF-ESTEEM
Achievement, mastery, recognition

SOCIAL NEEDS
Friends, family, community

SAFETY NEEDS
Security, structure, stability

PHYSICAL NEEDS
Shelter, warmth, food, water

Figure 6.1: Maslow's hierarchy of needs

Maslow's pyramid spans five categories that can be boiled down to three essentials: the need for food, shelter, and safety, that is, basic requirements for survival; the need for family, friendship, and intimacy, which creates a sense of belonging, love, and acceptance; and, at the top of the pyramid, a need for self-esteem and "self-actualization," defined as the ability to pursue your interests, which may include charity and service to others. As Maslow succinctly put it, "What a man can be, he must be."

At first glance, Maslow's hierarchy of needs may seem unrelated to the discipline of investing. But if you define risk as *the failure to meet your needs (or goals)*, then the hierarchy of needs provides an elegantly straightforward way to think about how to order those goals and the consequences of falling short. Using Maslow's framework as inspiration, every investor can categorize and prioritize goals, as follows:

ESSENTIAL GOALS:

- *Safety and shelter*: the certainty of protection from anxiety or poverty. Risks include loss of employment, health issues, loss of life (as a risk to other family members), accidents, and so on.
- In order to meet your essential goals, you must construct a safety net that protects you from the variety of risks listed above, including extreme market volatility. In other words, you must achieve a certain level of *safety*.

IMPORTANT GOALS:

- *Thriving within a peer group*: this enables and facilitates the process of nurturing and supporting those who are important to you, including a spouse, your family, and peers.

- In order to meet your important goals, you must achieve a high probability of maintaining your current standard of living. In other words, you must achieve *stability*.

ASPIRATIONAL GOALS:

- A way to pursue your dreams and aspirations, including further education, starting or expanding a business, philanthropic giving, or other aspirational goals like travel.
- In order to meet your aspirational goals, you may have to allocate capital to projects that may be viewed as uneconomical or to investments that, in adverse circumstances, may result in catastrophic losses. Your pursuit of aspirational goals must therefore be sized appropriately to recognize the possibility that the capital invested in such idiosyncratic endeavors may be completely lost.

The way to get a handle on your goals, then, is to make a list; categorize them as *essential*, *important*, and *aspirational*; and quantify the cost by deconstructing each one into a series of cash flows.

Saving for retirement isn't your only goal, of course. Other financial goals include saving for a child's college education, buying a new car, purchasing or maintaining a vacation home, or starting a business. Different people will categorize the same types of goals in different categories. This prioritization depends on a variety of factors, such as your age, how much money you have relative to your needs, and the simple fact that one person's essentials may be another individual's aspirations.

Let's imagine that you have only one essential goal: to retire. Rather than turn to a retirement calculator and be led astray by potentially flawed assumptions, there is a simple alternative calculation for your Number that requires just a single, key assumption: that your investment return matches the rate of inflation. This assumption enables you to easily calculate *in today's dollars what you will need in the future*. It simplifies all of the calculations to a remarkable degree and also provides an important buffer against the negative effects of withdrawing money during market downturns.

An economist might call this approach "calculating in today's purchasing power" or "the constant purchasing power method." I call it the "zero discounting method" or "really simple retirement calculation." Every number is reduced to what you need today, and thus everything is directly comparable in purchasing power. An additional benefit of using this approach is that if you or your financial advisor wants to be more aggressive or more conservative in your assumptions, you will be able to adjust the calculation in a single place, at the very end. What could be simpler?

To illustrate the really simple retirement calculation in action, let's quantify the retirement goal. It requires us to understand only one simple equation, as follows:

NEST EGG REQUIRED TO RETIRE TODAY

(IN TODAY'S DOLLARS) = # OF YEARS IN RETIREMENT x HOW

MUCH YOU SPENT OVER THE PAST 12 MONTHS

To keep things simple, let's assume some round numbers:

- You are sixty-five and ready to retire.
- You plan to spend $100,000 annually in retirement.
- You will live to the age of ninety.

Therefore, in order to retire today and spend the next 25 years in a comfortable lifestyle, you need to have a total net worth determined by your annual spend ($100,000) multiplied by the number of years (25), or $2.5 million in today's dollars. If you want to spend $200,000 annually for the next 25 years, then you would need twice as much, or $5 million. Similarly, if you plan to spend only $50,000 a year, the number is $1.25 million.

What if instead you are 60 years old today and wants to call it quits at age 65—in five years' time? The beauty of the really simple retirement calculation is that this wrinkle doesn't complicate the math. Since we assume that savings are invested in a portfolio that matches inflation and thus earns the cost of living, when you do the calculation in the future the savings and spending needs are exactly equal. The upshot: if you are 60 and want to retire at 65, assuming all other variables are equal, you still need $2.5 million in today's dollars. The answer is the same.

One of the biggest benefits of conducting this cash flow exercise for all of your goals, not just retirement, is that it will provide you with a fairly good sense of whether your goals are realistic or unrealistic, in aggregate, given the financial resources at your disposal.

It's the cash that counts. As the character Mr. Micawber states in Charles Dickens's classic tale *David Copperfield*:

Annual income twenty pounds, annual expenditure nineteen six, result happiness.

Annual income twenty pounds, annual expenditure twenty pound ought and six, result misery.

Just as Dickens suggests, if you spend more than you earn every year—or, in this modern age of easy credit, if you accumulate excessive debt in the form of credit card balances or home equity loans—no investment or wealth management strategy can save your finances, unless you have exceptional luck. (Mr. Micawber, unfortunately, was not one of the fortunate ones: he is sent to debtors' prison.)

At any stage of life, a viable wealth management strategy depends on you being cash flow positive. That is why it is crucially important to work through such a calculation for yourself and your family, perhaps with the help of a financial advisor. Chances are that your current net worth is much less than your Number. This may be reasonable given the stage of life you are in or a solvable problem if you still have a few years to go before retirement. Once you have retired, alas, the options available to you other than cutting your costs become very limited.

Still, as with any cardinal rule, including the rule that you must remain cash flow positive, there are exceptions. For example, it may make long-term financial sense to spend more than you earn when you take a loan against what will become an important asset in the future—for example, a university or professional degree. Yet caution is in order: you must have sufficient means to stay the course and complete the educational objective, and the degree should be both professionally enriching and sufficiently marketable so that you can ultimately earn a return above both the actual cost and the opportunity cost of lost wages. Similarly, a case can be made for assuming a loan in order to take full advantage of your employer's 401(k) matching contributions, or to buy insurance that can help prevent a financial disaster.

On the other hand, sacrificing positive cash flow to fund entrepreneurial activities is especially risky, notwithstanding the mythology of the American entrepreneur who bets everything to realize a business vision. We will deconstruct some of these myths in a later chapter and discuss additional safeguards and strategies that maximize, or at least enhance, the probability of success of such ventures.

The truest test of a successful investing and wealth management strategy is whether it can effectively insulate your essential goals from the whims of the financial markets, while simultaneously positioning you to achieve important goals and preserving your opportunity to achieve aspirational goals. In addition, your optimal strategy should be easy to understand and provide clarity on the steps required to get back on track, should adverse circumstances prevail. As we shall see, the Wealth Allocation Framework strives to provide exactly that.

A NEW FRAMEWORK

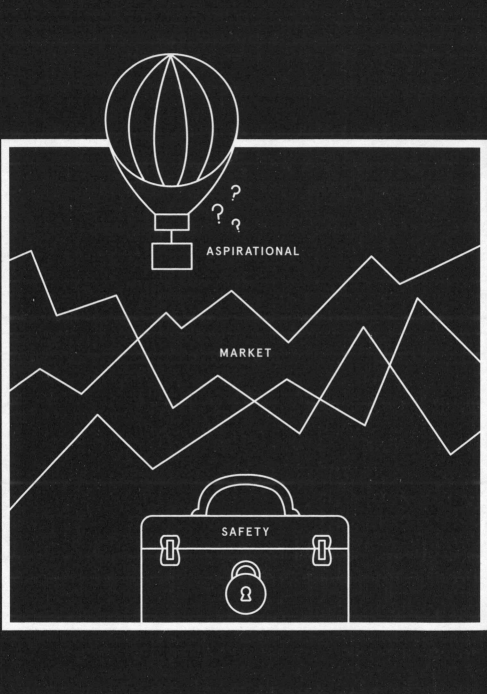

The Wealth Allocation Framework

What does the ideal investment portfolio look like? If you discuss your investments with a financial advisor on a regular basis, the conversation probably centers on the mix of stocks, bonds, and other assets that you own, as well as a variety of statistical measures of risk and return. If the market has moved up recently, perhaps your advisor has suggested rebalancing by selling some stocks and buying bonds. If there's an expectation that interest rates may rise, your advisor may suggest selling bonds or other fixed-income investments. If a manager or mutual fund is under-performing, your advisor may suggest selling it and buying another that has better performance. The larger context is likely driven by recent performance, with a focus on volatility as the risk measure.

Think about it carefully for a minute. I bet this experience leaves you feeling unsatisfied or, at best, wondering if there isn't more to the story. The framework for advisory discussions like these is the legacy of modern portfolio theory, first introduced in the now-famous 1952 paper by Harry Markowitz. According to the principles of the theory, there are two key dimensions of risk. The first is volatility (measured by standard deviation in statistical parlance), which describes the amount that the price of a security fluctuates over time. The second is correlation, which quantifies how securities move in relation to each other and helps determine the stability of portfolio returns. "Optimized" portfolios, according to the theory, are based on a combination of securities appropriately sized relative to each other to make some of the risk disappear without sacrificing returns. Many investors know these principles by name: diversification and asset allocation.

Today we are all disciples of Harry Markowitz. When you walk into any financial advisor's office, the reports presented to you will no doubt feature an "efficient frontier," a graphic representation of optimized portfolios at various targeted levels of return, and a suggested asset allocation, the latter in pie chart form, which, as we have discussed, tends to anchor your advisory relationship in a misguided quest to beat the market.

The near-universal acceptance of the Markowitz mean-variance framework is reflected in the financial industry's continuing use of the volatility of returns to define investment risk, despite a variety of obvious shortcomings. For starters, statistics teaches us that variance is a symmetrical risk measure, one that does not distinguish between upside moves and downside moves. A fund manager who has a few upside surprises in his portfolio should surely not be penalized the same way as a manager who ends up owning a few duds!

So why might you be feeling unsatisfied? One reason is that reducing the complexity of risk to a number is fraught with peril, as behavioral psychologists Daniel Kahneman and Amos Tversky have shown. In an editorial aptly entitled "The Myth of Risk Attitudes," Kahneman points out: "It is common ground in the industry . . . that the task of a financial advisor is to find a portfolio that fits a number: the investor's 'attitude to risk.' My purpose, here, is to suggest that there is no such thing."

Kahneman goes on to explain:

A central claim of prospect theory is that people are not consistently risk averse. Yes, they are much more sensitive to losses than to gains. But they are also risk seeking, both in their attraction to long shots and in their willingness to gamble when faced with a near-certain loss. To complicate things further, we know that people do not have a global view of their assets. They hold separate mental accounts and are much more willing to gamble from some of the accounts than others. To understand an individual's complex attitudes toward risk, we must know both the size of the loss that may destabilize them and the amount they are willing to put into play for a chance to achieve large gains.

Perhaps more tangibly, the standard measure of portfolio risk seems to have gotten divorced from the notion of consequences. As private investor Robert Jeffrey insightfully wrote in a 1984 paper, volatility alone is "simply a benign statistical probability." The true risk of investing, he argued, "is that [a portfolio] might not provide its owner, either during the interim or at some terminal date or both, with the cash he requires to make essential outlays." Thus what matters is not the volatility of a security, according to Jeffrey, *but its price at the time you need to sell it to meet an obligation.* Risk is therefore not simply "what happens" in the abstract but rather the impact of what happens—the "event risk"—on your ability to generate cash flow when you need it.

Furthermore, the very concept of "efficient" portfolios is unsatisfactory when applied to the objective of wealth creation. Since risk and return are two sides of the same coin, creating a well-diversified portfolio that seeks to eliminate all of the risk that can be diversified away might not necessarily be a good thing. If you have an information advantage—deep industry knowledge in a particular area, for example—your financial strategy should enable you to leverage this expertise to create wealth, without jeopardizing your living standard. Likewise, if your aspirations include launching a business or pursuing a vocation that is essential to your personal fulfillment and happiness, your wealth management strategy should work to accommodate this objective.

Perhaps most important, the standard implementation of modern portfolio theory seems to inadequately account for the possibility of extreme adverse market moves, which, as we have seen in prior chapters, occur with alarming frequency. The distinction between true "uncertainty" and "risk," as Markowitz came to define it, is in fact crucial for investors. One of the first scholars to carefully differentiate the two was University of Chicago economics professor Frank Knight, an iconoclast and firm believer in free markets. In his famous 1921 book, *Risk, Uncertainty and Profit*, Knight described risk as a "known chance" that is "measurable," and uncertainty, which is "unknowable" and thus "unmeasurable."

This distinction was further articulated decades later by Benoit Mandelbrot, a brilliant mathematician who is best remembered today for his pioneering work in fractal geometry, the study of unevenly contoured shapes, a discipline that he applied to a variety of subjects, including finance. In a famous paper published in 1963, he argued that the underlying dynamics of financial markets were "unpredictable, wild and woolly" and were thus not amenable to conventional statistical analysis. The volatility of markets is not just hard to measure, he argued, but in fact it is *infinite*. Financial markets, like floods and hurricanes, are inherently unpredictable. They are not "mildly random but *wildly* random."

It would take several decades, a paradigm shifting book, and a cataclysmic market correction for the arguments against traditional statistical optimization models to go mainstream. The credit goes to Nassim

Nicholas Taleb, author of *The Black Swan: The Impact of the Highly Improbable*. The options trader turned literary essayist and philosopher was born in Lebanon, and thus had firsthand experience of risk (of the life-or-death variety) from an early age. As defined by Taleb, a "black swan" event possesses three characteristics. First, the event is rare, an outlier, and by extension not predictable *ex ante*. Second, the event makes an extreme impact. And third, human nature being what it is, the event appears, in retrospect, to be both explainable and predictable.

Taleb and Mandelbrot make similar but distinct points. Mandelbrot argues against the very idea that we can, through optimization, tune the risk of a portfolio of investments, since market dynamics are uncertain and the variance (or "risk") is in fact infinite. Taleb argues that big, unexpected events determine history and the course of our lives, often with devastating impact. However, these "black swan" events appear, in retrospect, to be explainable and manageable, and are reinterpreted by self-serving experts as such.

Regardless of your own aspirations, your wealth management strategy and framework for managing risk must accommodate competing and sometimes incompatible objectives. You might wish to launch a business, while also creating a strategy to provide a financial safety net in the event of extreme downside market moves. Such goals may seem impossibly incongruous, but they need not be. As we've seen, every individual or family needs a framework that delivers on three principal objectives:

- The certainty of protection from anxiety and poverty, or *safety*.
- A high probability of maintaining your standard of living, or *stability*.
- The possibility of achieving upward wealth mobility and creating the potential to meet your *aspirations*.

These three seemingly straightforward objectives form the foundation of the *Wealth Allocation Framework*, an approach to managing wealth that combines modern portfolio theory's teachings on asset allocation and diversification with key insights from behavioral finance. It is, in fact, in Kahneman and Tversky's seminal paper on Prospect Theory that people's consideration of probable outcomes (certainty, probability, or possibility) in their decision making was discussed in the context of financial gambles.

Most important, the Wealth Allocation Framework provides a pragmatic, multidimensional approach to managing risk *in relation to your goals*. In the Wealth Allocation Framework, risk management addresses both quantifiable risk within the Markowitz framework and true uncertainty as defined by Knight and Mandelbrot. This process, called *risk allocation*, is achieved by creating three distinct risk buckets to support each of the corresponding three key objectives of your wealth management strategy.

The risk buckets, shown in Figure 7.1, can be summarized as follows:

- *Personal Risk*: You must protect yourself from the anxiety of a dramatic decrease in your standard of living. Thus, you must immunize yourself from personal risk: the devastating impact of not being able to meet your essential cash needs, regardless of the performance of financial markets.
- *Market Risk*: You must maintain your lifestyle by earning a rate of return in the financial markets that is comparable to the increase in the cost of living. Thus you will probably have to take on market risk. This is the risk, according to Markowitz, that cannot be diversified away through portfolio optimization.

- *Aspirational Risk*: In order to create the possibility of wealth creation and wealth mobility, or to fulfill your aspirational goals, you may decide to allocate capital to investments or business ventures that involve idiosyncratic risk and the potential for substantial capital gain or loss.

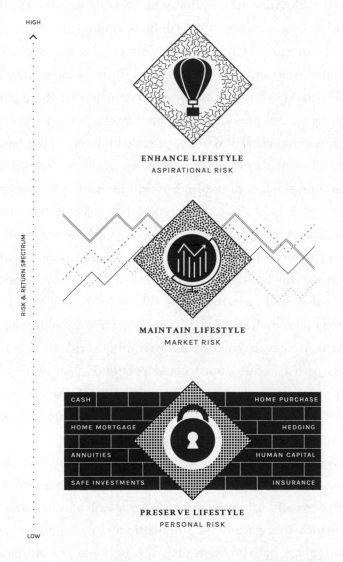

Figure 7.1: The three dimensions of the risk-return trade-off

Because of its diversified nature, the market risk bucket is about *statistically quantifiable risk*—the focus of Markowitz's pioneering work. The safety and aspirational portfolios, on the other hand, *are about the risk and opportunity of uncertain outcomes*, the focus of Knight and Mandelbrot, among others.

In the Wealth Allocation Framework, risk allocation—that is, the allocation of your assets and liabilities among the three risk buckets—is more important than, and in fact must precede, both the selection of assets and the selection of investments and managers.

The Wealth Allocation Framework recognizes that there is no free lunch. Assets that provide safety and have the potential to hold their value in a market crash will not provide high return potential. Therefore, investments allocated to the personal risk bucket will be selected to limit the loss of wealth but will probably yield below-market returns. Allocations to the market risk bucket will provide risk-adjusted market returns, in accordance with the diversification principles of modern portfolio theory. Finally, allocations to the aspirational risk bucket should be selected to yield above-market returns, but they will carry the risk of substantial loss of capital.

In this manner, each of the three core objectives of your wealth management strategy is assigned its own unique risk profile and requires its own carefully constructed portfolio: a *safety portfolio* consisting of protective assets; a *market portfolio* with the objective of stability for the long term; and an *aspirational portfolio* to help you generate wealth to achieve your aspirational goals.

The Wealth Allocation Framework thus builds upon Markowitz's legacy and incorporates, within a single, unifying framework, all of your assets and liabilities: not only your cash and investment portfolio, which are typically the singular focus of a traditional advisory relationship, but also assets such as your home or a business.

Because the Wealth Allocation Framework shifts the focus from the abstract performance of markets to your goals and corresponding risks, a key step is *getting to the right risk allocation*: determining how much risk you are currently taking, and how much risk you in fact *need to take or mitigate*, in order to maximize the probability that you will achieve your investment goals.

Thanks to those easily recognizable pie charts supplied by your financial advisor or brokerage firm, you are no doubt aware of the current or proposed asset allocation of your investment portfolio. But how do you determine your current and proposed *risk allocation*?

To begin the process, you (with your financial advisor) should construct an approximate snapshot of your current *risk allocation*. It is a relatively simple but critical process that involves placing all of your assets and liabilities in the appropriate safety, market, or aspirational buckets. Here are a few ground rules:

Assuming you are not overly concentrated in a stock, sector, country, or asset class, most of your liquid investments will likely be allocated to the market bucket.

If, however, an investment provides *safety and is thus characterized by below-market risk*, then it belongs in the safety bucket and will likely provide below-market returns.

Finally, if an investment *has the potential for above-market returns*, it must also possess above-market risk, and thus belongs in the aspirational bucket. Any concentrated or leveraged positions also belong in the aspirational bucket.

Although it is not difficult to objectively assess the suitability of different assets and securities for each risk bucket, *you must consider both the risk and return profile of the investment and the purpose it serves in your portfolio to determine the appropriate placement*. This is why different investors may sometimes place the same security in different buckets: placement depends on how the security is being used in the portfolio. As noted above, the three-bucket Wealth Allocation Framework provides no free lunch. As such, there are only three categories for your assets: low-risk with low return; market risk with market return; and high return potential with high risk. There is, alas, no low-risk, high-return bucket!

Of course, you may come across or already own an asset that has a lot of risk but very little return potential. The solution in most cases is simple: sell it. Similarly, you may be very lucky or smart and conclude that you have an asset with very little risk and a high return potential. But, unless you are truly an expert investor with specialized knowledge, in most cases the best investment advice you can follow with regard to such an asset is to stop fooling yourself.

Working through the liability side of your personal balance sheet is similarly straightforward. All personal liabilities and debt should be allocated to the safety portfolio, where they reduce the size of your personal safety net. The only exceptions—non-recourse loans attached to specific investments—should be placed in the same buckets that hold those particular investments. In similar fashion, these loans will reduce the value of the corresponding asset.

Let's take a look at the nuances of these risk buckets and the categorization of assets within them.

Safety, or Protective, Bucket. Protecting your living standard means defending against a multitude of potentially devastating events, including the loss of a job, a major health problem, disability, even lawsuits. Catastrophic market crashes or country defaults also present clear and present threats to your personal wealth. But beyond these obvious risks lie more nuanced ones that depend on your lifestyle, life stage, and market conditions. For example, withdrawing a fixed amount of money each year can have adverse consequences in a declining market. Falling markets might also accelerate the risk of outliving your assets. However, if you are at the peak of your earning capacity, you might be able to take on more risk than an individual who is approaching retirement.

Securities that provide some degree of stability or principal protection clearly fall into the safety bucket. These include cash, short-term Treasury bonds, short- and medium-duration Treasury inflation-protected securities (which provide inflation protection in exchange for a lower yield), principal-protected notes, certain types of annuities, and option strategies used for hedging purposes. Additional assets appropriate for the safety bucket include your primary residence, offset by mortgage debt, as we will explore in more detail.

Essentials such as insurance on your home and automobile, as well as catastrophe, disability, and life insurance, often have no intrinsic value, but they, too, are appropriate to include in your safety bucket. Although insurance policies deplete your safety net every year by consuming premiums, their true value will be evident when we introduce scenario analysis (more on that in Chapter 9). The role of insurance, after all, is to protect against low-probability events that would have a devastating impact on your financial picture or that of your dependents.

Finally, your human capital, or earnings potential, offset by any outstanding educational debt, also belongs in the safety bucket.

Market Bucket. Assets typically included in this risk bucket mirror those of a traditional portfolio allocated to stocks and bonds in accordance with modern portfolio theory. Nearly all conventional equity and fixed-income securities fall into the market bucket, as long as they are sized appropriately as part of your diversification strategy. Alternative investments, such as a fund of hedge funds or commodity or real estate funds, may also belong in the market bucket if these investments are held for diversification purposes and the relatively higher fees and transaction costs, liquidity constraints, and manager risks associated with these investments are in some way mitigated or diversified. Fixed-income securities with moderate interest rate or credit risk belong here, too. However, as noted earlier, short-term Treasuries—those with no credit risk and very little risk of capital loss if interest rates rise—should be treated as cash equivalents and thus belong in the safety bucket.

Aspirational Bucket. This bucket is motivated by the observation that sizable wealth creation requires leverage and concentration of specific assets, even if these characteristics are recognized as "inefficient" within the framework of modern portfolio theory. Assets in this bucket are riskier than the market in general and include the possibility of catastrophic failure and loss of principal.

More often than not, investors may have sizable aspirational assets as a consequence of holding company stock and stock options from the company where they work, or by virtue of owning a business. Investors may underestimate the riskiness of these assets because of their familiarity, which can lead to overconfidence and the illusion of control.

Assets that fall into the aspirational bucket include venture capital and early-stage "angel" investments, as well as family-owned businesses that make up a significant portion of an individual's net worth. In addition, the aspirational bucket includes executive stock options, concentrated stock positions, single-manager hedge funds, leveraged investments in real estate, and opportunistic call option instruments.

The Wealth Allocation Framework is carefully designed to be logical, intuitive, and simple to understand. The key to risk allocation is not only understanding the particular characteristics of your various assets but also thinking carefully about the role they play in your portfolio. In the next chapter, we'll work through the nuances of integrating major assets into the Wealth Allocation Framework, from your home or a business to gold, hedge funds, and even concentrated stock positions and stock options. We'll also discuss the right way to think about, and measure, your progress.

Within the Wealth Allocation Framework, this novel exercise in risk and resource management can be illuminating—and surprising.

Digging Deeper

When it comes to investing, understanding what you own, and why you own it, is one of the most crucial determinants of success. Yet many investors treat their portfolios like a dusty attic: a place to hold items bought or inherited long ago, some with value but others that probably no longer fit their purpose.

At the same time, investors are apt to overlook the totality of their personal balance sheet when constructing and managing their wealth management strategy, focusing instead on the performance of their liquid assets. This limited sight line can in part be explained by the focus on modern portfolio theory, which addresses the risk and return characteristics of assets like stocks and bonds but is less helpful for assessing and integrating other types of holdings, such as a home, stock options, a business, or even lifetime earnings potential, or "human capital," which is arguably one of your most important assets.

The Wealth Allocation Framework accommodates all of these aspects of your financial life, enabling you to marshal your entire personal balance sheet in support of your goals. But successful implementation depends on properly classifying everything you own within the three distinct risk buckets described in the previous chapter. To help guide this process, you must analyze *all of your assets and ascertain why you own them*. As we shall see, both the individual risk and return characteristics and the ultimate purpose for owning each asset are what determine its placement in the appropriate risk bucket—and that, in turn, will help determine the size of the position and the ultimate form of ownership.

In many cases, the struggle to classify an asset results from preconceptions or from a deep, almost blinding, familiarity with it: the things you know best are often sizable and thus of relatively high importance within your overall financial picture. That makes proper classification all the more important.

A standard classification of assets and liabilities in accordance with the Wealth Allocation Framework is shown in Figure 8.1.

In the pages that follow, we'll examine in detail several commonly held yet difficult-to-classify assets and strategies:

- Private businesses
- Concentrated stock and stock options
- Real estate
- Gold
- Hedge funds, private equity, and other alternative investments
- Currency trading
- Human capital
- Cash

Our primary focus in this chapter will not be to explain the nuances and the possible pitfalls of these sometimes sophisticated strategies in detail. Rather, we will explain which risk bucket these strategies fall into and why, so that you can correctly create a comprehensive risk allocation statement consisting of your entire net worth.

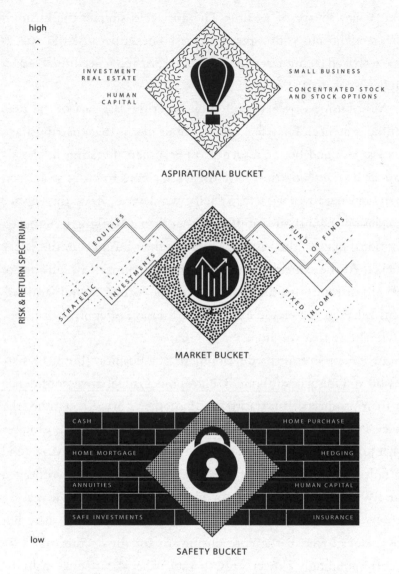

INVESTMENT
REAL ESTATE

HUMAN
CAPITAL

SMALL BUSINESS

CONCENTRATED STOCK
AND STOCK OPTIONS

ASPIRATIONAL BUCKET

RISK & RETURN SPECTRUM

EQUITIES

STRATEGIC   INVESTMENTS

FUND OF FUNDS

FIXED INCOME

MARKET BUCKET

CASH

HOME MORTGAGE

ANNUITIES

SAFE INVESTMENTS

HOME PURCHASE

HEDGING

HUMAN CAPITAL

INSURANCE

SAFETY BUCKET

high

low

Figure 8.1: Classification of assets and liabilities in the Wealth Allocation Framework

PRIVATE BUSINESSES

Say you're a successful business owner. How exactly should you deal with a profitable enterprise that is growing steadily, at per-haps 20 percent to 30 percent a year, and has been, and still is, your major source of wealth? The answer is simple: the business goes straight into your aspirational risk bucket because the asset is characterized by higher-than-market return and is accompanied by higher-than-market risk.

Most business owners will choke over the last part of the preceding sentence. They feel, not without merit, that their business has less risk and better return prospects than investing in the financial markets, and they have the track record to prove it. In fact, many business owners, left to their own devices, draw the *opposite* conclusion about their company: rather than classifying it in the aspirational bucket, they attempt to place their business in the safety bucket. At the same time, they estimate a continued high rate of growth or return for the business into the future. Sound familiar? This behavior is a classic example of "illusion of control," the behavioral trap that we discussed in Chapter 2.

At some point in the development of a business (both the successful and unsuccessful ones!), entrepreneurs feel great confidence in their prospects. But statistics tell another story. Over time, the success stories represent only a small minority of the businesses with high-growth potential that are actually launched. Most tend to fail, and high rates of return simply do not come without a variety of risks, including embedded leverage. Firms that mature achieve a certain size, which helps mitigate many of the risks, but any reduced risk in the core business is usually accompanied by a correspondingly slower growth rate. The sweet spot—a high-growth company with low business risk—is usually a transient phenomenon and hard to identify a priori.

Nonetheless, entrepreneurs in the process of building a business often have great optimism about the future, great confidence in their judgment and abilities, and considerable pride in their track record. That is perhaps ironic, since most business owners do recognize that, as they become more successful, they must increasingly protect themselves from a variety of risks, including all of the people who come out of the woodwork looking for a piece of the pie: competitors who want to take away market share; patent trolls who want a share of the revenue; lawyers representing disgruntled customers seeking disproportionate damages; suppliers who over-promise and under-deliver; customers who take delivery but do not pay . . . the list goes on.

These risks aren't the only reasons that a business belongs in the aspirational bucket. The cliché of comparing competitive business with war is not without merit. Most business owners always feel that they are at an inflection point, that the right decisions and execution by their company will allow them to capitalize on great opportunity, while the wrong decisions can sink them. In short, the relentless presence of embedded risk cannot be understated.

Finally, it's worth noting that a large holding such as a business, by virtue of its concentration, raises the risk exposure of your overall portfolio. If the company's fortunes decline or, worse, if it ceases to exist, the resulting decline in the position will naturally have a disproportionately adverse impact on your overall wealth. Such concentration of holdings (and risk) is ever present if you are a business owner.

CONCENTRATED STOCK AND EXECUTIVE STOCK OPTIONS

Many successful executives find themselves in the fortunate situation of holding oversized positions in stock and stock options from the companies where they work. Small to midsize companies that grow into larger firms over time through organic growth, mergers, or acquisitions have been a primary source of wealth for many in the corporate world, not just those in Silicon Valley.

Most executives understand objectively that holding large, concentrated positions of employer stock and stock options is a fundamentally risky proposition. Still, executives often have difficulty diversifying these positions for a variety of reasons that include: comfort and familiarity with the business; a sense of loyalty to the company and fear of being viewed as disloyal; good visibility into the day-to-day workings of the organization; aversion to paying the taxes that would be due along with any sale; and the strong historical growth record of the company, coupled with a perception that future prospects are just as bright.

Modern portfolio theory's treatment of concentrated positions is simplistic: sell them and invest the proceeds in a diversified portfolio. The Wealth Allocation Framework is more nuanced. The idea is to work out an appropriate percentage of the position that you may retain, in order to balance allocations to the three risk buckets while remaining consistent with your goals and objectives.

The approach is straightforward: because company stock and stock options are highly leveraged and/or concentrated investments, they belong in the aspirational risk bucket. If any of the stock or stock options can be hedged, however, then, depending on the structure of the hedge, the hedged portion would move to the personal or market risk bucket.

After the technology stock crash of 2000 and the financial crisis of 2008, many executives found that their company stock and stock options, even in some blue-chip Fortune 500 companies, became worthless. Alas, you simply cannot disentangle the high-risk component from high-returning assets like concentrated stock and stock options. Nor should you count on these assets to achieve essential goals like funding your retirement. For these reasons, assets such as employer stock and stock options, generally speaking, belong in the aspirational bucket.

REAL ESTATE

Land and property have traditionally been thought of as great sources of wealth and safety. Until recently, they were also sizable elements and strong performers in many investors' portfolios, especially if a rapidly appreciating primary residence is factored into the equation. However, the crash of 2008 has changed many of these perceptions—at least for this generation of investors.

Let's start with what is likely to be your most important asset: your home. When you make a 5 to 20 percent down payment, assume a mortgage, and take possession of your primary home, you are taking on what is likely to be the biggest, most leveraged, and highly concentrated investment you will ever make. In a way this is odd, since the role of a primary home is not to serve as a speculative, leveraged real estate investment but rather to provide stability for your family over at least a generation. For this reason, it is sensible to make a reasonably large down payment and endeavor to pay off your mortgage over time, thus reducing the leverage in that investment.

As many home owners now know all too well, the benefits of rapid home price appreciation are illusory. For starters, it's next to impossible to profit during boom cycles: even if you sell your home when prices are high, you still have to buy *another home at a similarly inflated price* (you must live somewhere, after all!). Renting till the market corrects is akin to trying to time the market, which is particularly dangerous when the market cycle can be several decades long. Only when you retire and move to a smaller home, or inherit a home and flip it, can you profit from the irrational exuberance of house prices.

Over much longer periods, the story isn't much better. As we showed in Chapter 3, four hundred years of price data on homes in the Dutch city of Amsterdam suggest that, *over the long haul, real estate merely grows at or just slightly above the rate of inflation.*

For these reasons, a sensible primary home, together with a mortgage on the property, should be allocated to the personal risk bucket: homes are safety assets, not speculative investments. Conversely, a rental property such as a condominium might belong in either the market risk bucket or the aspirational risk bucket, depending on the amount of leverage. If a loan taken against the property is small and manageable and the property location is relatively stable, then the condo belongs in the market risk bucket, where it diversifies the risk and return characteristics of an overall investment portfolio. If the property is instead highly leveraged, or it is a speculative bet located in an area that is "filled with potential," as a real estate agent might say, then the property belongs instead in the aspirational risk bucket.

Similarly, a real estate investment trust (REIT) or a real estate fund structured as a limited partnership may belong in the market risk bucket, if it is a small part of a large, diversified portfolio, or it might belong in the aspirational bucket, if it is a large position in a single fund.

GOLD

Many of us relate to gold as a store of value and a source of safety in uncertain times. Other investors argue with considerable logic that gold at best keeps up with inflation and is a beneficiary of a sort of "social bubble": it is intrinsically valuable only because enough other people are fooled for a time into thinking it has value. This much is certain: gold prices are subject to massive supply-and-demand bubbles that often lead individual investors seeking a safe haven to buy gold at vastly inflated prices, only to suffer considerable losses.

As with any asset, the reason you hold gold, the size of your position relative to your portfolio, and your choice of how you hold the precious metal are what determine its appropriate placement within your *risk allocation*.

When seeking safety from economic collapse, war, or the debasement of paper currencies, it might be best to hold physical gold. Holding gold as a disaster hedge is a long-term investment; as such, it may make sense to accumulate the asset gradually and hold it for a lifetime. Historical data suggest that, over the long term, physical gold should yield a return consistent with inflation. Thus gold held for safety belongs in the personal risk bucket.

Yet gold also provides diversification benefits. Over the long term, as part of a diversified investment portfolio, it might be prudent to own an appropriately sized position in a gold mutual fund or exchange-traded fund, or even gold stocks that provide leveraged exposure to the spot gold price. Thus gold held for the diversification benefit belongs in the market bucket.

Similar arguments can be made with respect to diamonds and art. The valuations of these investments far exceed their intrinsic value, but such "social bubbles" may last for multiple centuries. Therefore, for an astute investor, these holdings can serve as excellent stores of value over a lifetime. Still, such investments are clearly speculative and belong in the aspirational bucket.

HEDGE FUNDS, PRIVATE EQUITY, AND OTHER ALTERNATIVE INVESTMENTS

Markowitz's framework emphasized the construction of efficient portfolios that diversified away the idiosyncratic risk, leaving only broad exposure to the market that could not be diversified away.

In recent years, nontraditional investments such as hedge funds, private equity, futures, commodities, and even foreign exchange have become integral components of the investment portfolios of many endowments, foundations, institutional investors, and ultra-high-net-worth individuals and families. More recently, innovations in the fund industry, such as nontraditional mutual funds, have made several of these strategies available to the vast majority of investors. Their appropriate placement within your risk allocation depends on both the particular risk-return characteristics of the alternative investments you hold and the role they play in your portfolio: whether it's for hedging, diversification, or a pure absolute return strategy.

Hedge funds are partnerships that have certain participation restrictions. You need a certain minimum net worth and sophistication in order to be eligible to invest. In turn, hedge fund managers have fewer investing constraints and regulations than do mutual fund managers. A common strategy employed by hedge funds for leveraging a manager's skill, while simultaneously reducing market risk, is called long-short investing. In order to measure a manager's skill, we need to understand the concepts of alpha and beta.

Alpha and Beta

When you buy a market index, you buy a good representation of the entire market. This gives you market return subject to market volatility.

When you invest in an actively managed fund, its return and risk come from two sources. The first comes from its exposure to the general market—we call this systematic risk and measure it through a quantity called market beta. The second comes from the choices the manager makes, that is, his or her particular picks. The excess return from these actions is idiosyncratic, in other words it is dependent on a manager's skill and in general is uncorrelated to the return of the general market. This excess return (positive or negative) is manager alpha.

An index that is representative of the market, the benchmark, has a beta of 1 and an alpha of 0 by definition. A portfolio with a beta of 0.5 would mean that the portfolio should move (return and volatility) about half as much as the underlying market and a beta of 2.0 would imply twice the movement.

An active manager with all assets invested in the equity market will, in general, have a beta close to 1 and then some alpha based on his or her skill or luck. This would mean that, if the general market, let us say the S&P 500 index, went up by 10 percent, and the fund went up by 12 percent, one would attribute 10 percent of the gain to the fund's general exposure to the equity markets and 2 percent to the manager's alpha. This would also be true if the index went down by 10 percent but the fund went down only 8 percent. Of course, alpha can be either positive or negative—so a manager with a −2 percent alpha would cause the fund to under-perform the index and be up only 8 percent or down 12 percent in the two market scenarios just discussed.

Markets, as we have repeatedly stated, are subject to large fluctuations. Returns due to exposure to the markets (beta) can vary greatly year to year. Economic valuations cause markets to mean-revert, so large gains eventually lead to sharp corrections and vice versa, and returns due to beta average out over time. Our analysis of global markets in Chapter 3 demonstrates, in fact, that global returns rewarded the long-term investor with a net return of 1 percent to 5 percent above inflation. Alpha, the source of return from a manager's stock selection process, should be uncorrelated to the general return of the market. Should the manager's choices turn out to be wrong on both the long and the short side, the effects of this embedded leverage will magnify the pain. This was why Odean and Barber's analysis of self-directed investors, discussed in Chapter 1, was so clever. Those self-directed investors had an alpha of −9 percent. Alpha is about relative performance!

One of the insights of the endowment model of investing, pioneered by David Swensen at Yale University (an approach that we will explore in detail in Chapter 11), is that one can get exposure to the general market quite cheaply (say, through equity futures or index funds), and one should pay managers only for the return generated by their skill, that is, alpha. There are three decisions equity managers can make: how much exposure they want to the market at any given time, what specific stocks they choose for the fund, and how they size them.

The first decision is the asset allocation decision: How much of a fund's capital should be exposed to the market? Obviously, if they like the market, they will maximize their equity exposure, while in the extreme case that they expect the market to go down they could exit the market and sit out. Thus, a long-only fund manager would be able to vary the fund's exposure from 0 percent to 100 percent. Both of these decisions can be sources of positive or negative alpha.

Long-Short Funds

A long-short fund provides more flexibility to the manager than just a long fund. It allows—as its name implies—a manager to short the market, that is, sell stocks the fund does not own and buy them back later. This is clearly a bet that the stock price will go down between the two transactions and is more aggressive than just going to cash. By buying stocks that a manager thinks are undervalued and selling stocks short that the manager thinks are overvalued, the long-short fund manager can vary both the fund's exposure to general market movements and the amount of capital allocated to their stock picks. The combination of going both long and short also allows the manager to lower or hedge the fund's systematic exposure or risk—or, simply put, its net exposure to the general market.

For example, a fund that was long 130 percent (of the manager's favorite stocks) but short 30 percent (of stocks the manager thinks are overpriced) would have systematic market exposure of 100 percent (beta of approximately 1) but 160 percent of the fund's capital would be invested in stock selection—thus leveraging up any eventual positive or negative alpha. At another time, the manager could be long 90 percent and short 60 percent, resulting in a market exposure of just 30 percent, but with 150 percent of the capital exposed to his or her stock selection skills.

An extreme variation would be to go long and short the same amount, say 100 percent long and 100 percent short, which would give the fund beta of 0 and make 200 percent of the capital dependent on the manager's alpha. This would be a market neutral fund, where the net exposure to systematic market movements is zero, and the manager can vary the total capital exposed to specific stock picks, depending on his or her conviction, without caring if the broad market goes up or down.

A long-short strategy thus reduces a fund's exposure to market beta and magnifies exposure to a fund manager's alpha. The theory is that since beta can be acquired in a portfolio (or a fund) rather cheaply, say, by indexing, why would you pay a manager for it? Skilled managers should be paid mostly for their alpha, so a strategy that reduces beta exposure and increases alpha can be a beneficial arrangement for both the investor and a highly skilled manager, who would charge higher than standard fees for this hard-to-obtain, uncorrelated, idiosyncratic return.

A broad-based portfolio of hedge funds that is diversified across different managers and investment strategies could be an attractive addition to the market portfolio. Such an allocation would belong in the market bucket. A common question is: Where does an investment in a single hedge fund manager belong? Many feel that their hedge fund investment is an aspirational investment. This may be true from a risk-return point of view: the fund manager may provide an outsized return or alternatively just take outsized risk and blow up. Sized appropriately as part of a diversified portfolio, such an investment, however exotic, still is just part of the market bucket. Aspirational investments require concentration and leverage to create a major impact on the total wealth of an individual or institution. This sizing up is generally not prudent. In reality, the hedge fund is usually an aspirational investment for the hedge fund manager. For all others, it is a different, sometimes less correlated way of getting market exposure (beta) and manager skill (alpha).

PRIVATE EQUITY

Another variation on extracting return from the equity market is private equity. The strategy aims to deliver excess returns by identifying public companies that are distressed or have fat balance sheets and can be taken private for restructuring. To be successful, private equity managers need long-term capital from investors who seek excess return, in exchange for investing over a long time horizon and accepting illiquidity.

The nature of private equity is unique. Investors must commit to making a series of pre-specified funding commitments to the manager, known as capital calls. Armed with the capital, private equity managers then look for takeover targets. With complete control, they take the company private, substantially restructure it, and pay investors back along the way through distributions in the form of large, special dividends. The goal is to seek a public offering or convince a larger company to buy the restructured entity, at which point investors earn a major payout.

A typical private equity fund has a three-year investment period and a ten-to-twelve-year total life. In order to compensate, in part, for the long time horizon and illiquidity of the capital committed, returns from such a strategy are expected to be considerably higher than those achieved by simply taking minority stakes in publicly traded companies via the equity market. Target returns for private equity are typically 5 to 10 percent a year above public markets.

Private equity investments, although illiquid, typically belong in the market bucket.

CURRENCY TRADING

A similar range of outcomes applies to foreign exchange. A pure currency hedge—applied not just to an investment portfolio but also possibly to real estate or business contracts—would have an underlying cost and belongs in the safety bucket. Yet a currency trading fund consisting of a portfolio of different currency positions can also serve as a diversifier—in which case, as a small percentage of a diversified portfolio, it might belong in the market bucket. On the other hand, a speculative foreign exchange position naturally carries the risk of loss of principal and should clearly be categorized in the aspirational bucket.

HUMAN CAPITAL

Although your earning potential is not accounted for in a typical statement of net worth, it is a key component of your financial life. Human capital often requires a considerable investment in education or apprenticeship at an early stage that, over the course of your lifetime, translates into financial assets through income and other earnings. In the latter stage of life, the cycle is reversed once again, and financial assets will be consumed in order to maintain your lifestyle. In the next chapter, we will describe how both your human capital and life-cycle stage may affect your risk allocation. Human capital, such as a basic skill or education, is part of everyone's safety net. A high degree of specialization becomes an aspirational asset—often requiring many years of investment before it pays out. A surgeon with a specialization in cardio-thoracic surgery, an accomplished architect, a stellar fund manager, a popular talk-show host, and a rock star all have human capital that can be placed in the aspirational bucket.

CASH

In the safety bucket, cash is reserved for liquidity and emergency needs—for example, by holding enough funds to cover six months to a few years of living expenditures. Cash in the other risk buckets serves an entirely different purpose: it's an opportunistic asset that can be deployed when the right investment comes along. This "patient capital" is best allocated to either the market or the aspirational bucket, depending on the target assets.

PERFORMANCE MEASUREMENT IN THE WEALTH ALLOCATION FRAMEWORK

What about performance measurement? Although the intent of the *risk allocation* process and the Wealth Allocation Framework more broadly is to shift your primary objective from "beating the market" to maximizing the probability that you will achieve your goals, you must still measure your progress objectively. There are two important and complementary ways to do so: first, you should use *separate performance benchmarks for each bucket*; and, second, you should *measure progress to your goals* in terms of the assets you have accumulated for each goal and your probabilities of achieving success.

With your financial advisor, you may be accustomed to

discussing the performance of your portfolio in comparison to conventional stock market benchmarks, or to a blended benchmark that represents a portfolio of stocks and bonds in, say, a 60:40 split. Within the Wealth Allocation Framework, the same concept applies, with an important caveat: *your return comparisons, risk measures, and benchmarks will be different for each of the three buckets.* Each risk bucket must be benchmarked against appropriate indices, because you should have very different performance expectations for the assets allocated to each bucket.

In the safety bucket, you are paying for security in the form of a reduced expected return. In the aspirational bucket, you are paying for the possibility of outsized returns in the form of additional idiosyncratic risk and a significant probability of capital loss. These two elements of your portfolio, in general, will behave differently than the market bucket. Thus assets in the safety bucket are a form of insurance, which you would expect to appreciate at below-market rates. In fact, though it may seem counterintuitive at first, you should actually aim for a zero rate of return after inflation for these assets. That's right, *no return.* Why? The answer is simple: if this portion of your portfolio were in fact to deliver a positive real return, you would most likely be taking risks that are not compatible with the purpose of this risk bucket: mitigating an existing risk or absolute safety.

Assets in the market bucket will be invested in accordance with modern portfolio theory. Performance can therefore be compared to standard market benchmarks, adjusted for the risk of the portfolio. When it comes to return expectations, it goes without saying that no investor can accurately predict what the long-term market return will be. Still, there is ample historical data to suggest that performance in the mid- to high single digits is a reasonable expectation as long as you are globally well diversified, are patient, and stay invested for the long term.

Assets in the aspirational bucket should significantly outperform standard market indices—when they perform at all. Indeed, when aspirational investments are successful, they have the potential to deliver several times the original investment. But when they do not perform, these investments may result in substantial loss of principal. The unique, binary nature of investment outcomes—either a big success or a smashing failure—makes aspirational investments difficult to benchmark. Apart from luck, the best risk mitigation strategy in this highest-risk bucket of your portfolio is to concentrate on areas of the market where you have expertise, an information edge, and/or control, and to identify the best minds in the business to collaborate or invest with.

So how do you know if your risk allocation and associated benchmarks for tracking performance are appropriate? This question can best be answered by viewing the expected performance of your entire risk allocation—and hence your portfolio itself—under a variety of market scenarios. Rather than undertaking complex market simulations, a handful of straightforward what-ifs is more than sufficient. For example, what if your market portfolio declines by 50 percent during an extended period of market stress, and your aspirational portfolio falls to zero? Could you sleep at night? Do you have sufficient liquidity and an adequate safety portfolio to carry you through? How would you feel about a longer period of moderate underperformance? Or substantial outperformance? Let's say, for example, that your market portfolio appreciates by 20 percent in a year and your aspirational portfolio doubles in value. Exactly how important is that upside? And just as crucially, are you comfortable with the risks you are taking to achieve that degree of outperformance?

In each of the scenarios above, how would you feel? What would you do?

OBJECTIVE-
DRIVEN
INVESTING

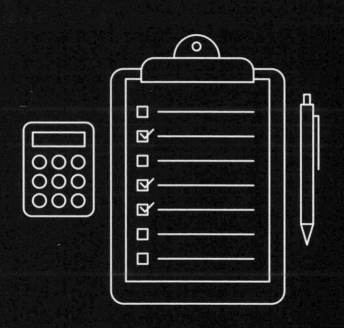

Seven Steps to Implementation

Let's pause and take stock. By now, I hope I have persuaded you that too many investors spend far too much time focused on the performance of the markets rather than on their preparedness for meeting their life's goals. As we have seen, this focus on markets leads to an unrelenting obsession with outperformance. And that misguided focus, in turn, can lead to all sorts of misbehaviors, many unintended, that are destructive to your wealth. The reality is that turning to financial markets for outsized wealth creation—the kind of riches that deliver upward wealth mobility—is simply a fool's errand, especially if you are putting your financial security at risk in the process.

There is, as I have argued, a much better way.

By organizing your financial life around what you hope to achieve for yourself and your family, you can secure the protection of an adequate safety net and ensure a reasonable probability that you will maintain your standard of living over time, while still creating the opportunity for aspirational goals like substantial wealth creation.

As with any new approach, the hardest part is figuring out how to get started. This chapter provides a complete road map for implementation, from goal setting to scenario testing. It is a comprehensive framework that can be suitably adapted for any wealth level and for most goals.

STEP 1: OUTLINE YOUR GOALS

When was the last time you actually wrote down your financial goals and aspirations? This may be something that you, like many people, have never done, at least not formally. This is the place to start. Document all of your goals and then categorize them as *essential, important,* and *aspirational.*

For example, a young couple at an early stage in their financial life might have a goal set that looks something like what you see in Figure 9.1.

On the other hand, a wealthy couple that has already retired may have only two goals as illustrated in Figure 9.2.

STEP 2: CONVERT YOUR GOALS INTO CASH FLOWS

Defining your goals as cash flows involves just two simple calculations. First, as demonstrated in Chapter 6, you can use the *zero discount method* to quantify the total amount needed *today* for virtually any goal using one easy formula:

SAVINGS REQUIRED THIS YEAR TOWARD A GOAL *N*

YEARS IN THE FUTURE.

= COST OF GOAL (IN TODAY'S DOLLARS)/*N*

ASSUMING YOU DO THIS EVERY YEAR!

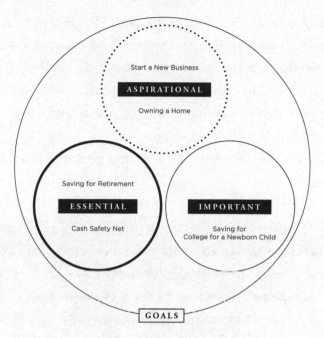

Figure 9.1: Goals for a young couple

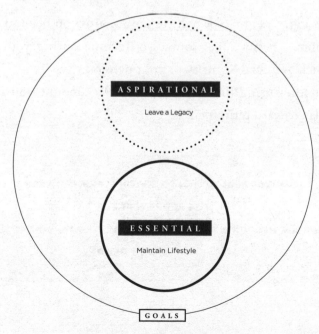

Figure 9.2: Goals for a wealthy couple

If you are saving for a college that costs \$100,000 today, and you will need to fund it in 10 years, then you need to invest a minimum of \$10,000 this year toward that goal, that is (\$100,000 ÷ 10). Next year, you repeat the same calculation, that is, re-estimate the cost of college, reduce this amount by the amount you have already saved, and divide by 9—and so on.

In the context of a retirement savings goal, the formula looks like this:

> **NEST EGG REQUIRED TO RETIRE TODAY (IN TODAY'S DOLLARS) =**
>
> **# OF YEARS IN RETIREMENT x HOW**
>
> **MUCH YOU SPENT OVER THE PAST 12 MONTHS**
>
> **x OPTIONAL ADJUSTMENT FACTOR**

(The adjustment factor reduces the amount you need to save by taking into account other sources of income during your retirement, such as Social Security or your pension.)

Therefore, using the same formula, the amount you need to save today toward retirement is:

> **SAVINGS REQUIRED (IN TODAY'S DOLLARS) PER YEAR**
>
> **FOR RETIREMENT =**
>
> **NEST EGG REQUIRED TO RETIRE TODAY (IN TODAY'S DOLLARS) /#**
>
> **OF YEARS LEFT TO RETIRE**

Creating a table that outlines both your savings allocated to each goal and the savings required annually to meet each goal will help you determine whether your goals are realistic.

This year-by-year analysis has the added advantage of enabling you to consider modifications to your lifestyle and expenses, if necessary. When it comes to remaining financially healthy, adaptability and flexibility are key.

Thus, assuming that the hypothetical couple's post-tax income is $150,000, their goals worksheet might look like what you see in Figure 9.3.

At this step, you should analyze whether your cash flows add up. Put another way: Is your spending too high? Are your goals too ambitious? Keep in mind that cash in-flows are generated from both financial assets and your "human capital" (that is, your job, if you are working). You should also examine cash out-flows: for example, will you need to withdraw money at any juncture or on a regular basis? If so, are your withdrawals likely to be a fixed or variable sum? Be aware that withdrawing a fixed amount of money every year, rather than a fixed percentage, can have adverse consequences in a declining market environment. More specific calculations will depend on your particular financial situation, tax status, the state you live in, your specific employment benefits, age, and so on. Most readers would benefit from consulting a financial advisor or financial planner to better understand how to incorporate these factors in their cash-flow analysis. However, the zero discounting method outlined in this chapter works as a surprisingly good initial estimate. Among other things, this method is simple to use and self-corrects as you recalculate and adjust every year.

As you work to quantify your goals as cash flows, you may wonder whether there is a preferred order for funding them. Intuitively, it might seem that funding *essential goals* should take precedence over saving and investing to achieve *important goals* and

	GOAL	LIFETIME NEED	CURRENT YEAR NEED OR TARGET SAVINGS
ESSENTIAL	**MAINTAIN LIFESTYLE**	**$100K** per year till retirement	spend **$100K** after tax per year
	CASH SAFETY NET	**$100K***2yrs = **$200K** (currently saved $50k)	shortfall **$150K** objective to put away **$20K** toward goal this year
	RETIREMENT	**$80K***25yrs = **$2MM** (of which $ 150k saved and invested in a diversified portfolio)	**$20K** pre-tax (max out 401k) i.e., equivalent to $15k post-tax payment
	PAY OFF COLLEGE LOANS	**$90K**	**$5K** interest payment only
IMPORTANT	**COLLEGE FOR NEWBORN CHILD**	**$80K** to **$200K** (depending on state vs private college)	**$5K**
	VACATION	**$2K** (this year only)	**$2K**
ASPIRATIONAL	**SAVINGS FOR CONDOMINIUM DOWN PAYMENT**	**$55K** (20% down +$15K for other costs) $10K saved	**$3K** ($45K still to be funded)
	TOTAL	Easy to add up. This will be a very large number—so do not even think of retiring early!	**$150K**

Figure 9.3: Sample goals worksheet

aspirational goals. Indeed, Maslow's hierarchy of needs, introduced in Chapter 6 as a starting point for organizing your goals, seems to suggest a natural ordering, funding essential goals first, then the important goals, then finally the aspirational goals. While this may be true, in many ways it is too simplistic.

Maslow's expression of human needs does indeed resonate with people across all cultures, as shown by recent research based on the Gallup World Poll, an illuminating survey on well-being that queried more than sixty thousand respondents from 123 countries. However, this study also found that people prefer to work toward many kinds of goals simultaneously. Human needs are "like vita- mins," as one of the researchers explained in an interview with the *Atlantic*: "we need them all."

So it goes with goal setting and *risk allocation* within the Wealth Allocation Framework. You don't need to have your safety net fully funded to begin the pursuit of an aspirational goal. It is a good strat- egy to start by funding your essential goals. But once you have a short-term safety net, you could also fund important and aspirational goals, thus building assets across your total portfolio simultaneously.

STEP 3: CREATE YOUR WEALTH ALLOCATION SNAPSHOT

Pulling together everything you own and everything you owe— your marketable securities, insurance policies, stock options, your home, and loans (such as a mortgage)—affords the opportunity to create a unified framework for managing your wealth. This is the step where you will organize your assets and liabilities across the personal risk, market risk, and aspirational risk buckets.

As described in the previous chapter, assets that provide safety and have the potential to hold their value in a market crash should be allocated to the safety portfolio. Assets that provide a risk-adjusted market return belong in the market portfolio. And assets that hold the potential for above-market returns, but also carry the potential for substantial loss of capital, should be allocated to the aspirational portfolio.

Over time the young couple's wealth allocation statement might evolve to look like Figures 9.4 and 9.5.

STEP 4: ASSESS YOUR RISK ALLOCATION

What is the "right" risk allocation across your safety, market, and aspirational portfolios? Alas, there are no exact answers, but there are good guidelines you can follow. Your optimal allocation depends on a variety of objective considerations and should strike a balance between factors such as your age and earning potential, your total current wealth, and the ratio of your assets to the amount you need to sustain your lifestyle. Subjective factors such as your goals and your ability to bear losses are also key factors.

It is often easier to identify how much risk is too much. You can approach the issue from two perspectives. A *subjective* approach captures your personal attitude toward risk: How should you invest so that you can sleep well at night? Some investors are simply more willing to take on risk than others to achieve their goals. On the flip side, an *objective* approach to risk is defined by your personal balance sheet and your financial ability to absorb losses.

A thorough analysis of your optimal risk allocation must therefore take into account both your *financial ability* and your *psychological ability* to bear losses. If you have no ability or desire to take on risk—or, conversely, you have a high tolerance and ability to take on risk—then either a conservative or an aggressive risk allocation may be warranted, defined by the degree to which you allocate assets on a relative basis to your safety portfolio or your aspirational portfolio.

GOAL	ACCOUNTS	% PORTFOLIO	PERSONAL	MARKET	ASPIRATIONAL
RETIREMENT	Protective	10%	100%	0%	0%
	IRA account 1	20%	40%	60%	0%
	IRA account 2	20%	30%	70%	0%
	Investment Account 1	10%	0%	100%	0%
	Employee Stocks & Stock options	10%	0%	0%	100%
CHILDREN'S EDUCATION	529 Plan 1	5%	50%	50%	0%
	529 Plan 2	5%	70%	30%	0%
	Investment Account 2	10%	0%	100%	0%
LEGACY WEALTH	Trust Account	10%	0%	80%	20%
Total Portfolio		100%	30%	58%	12%

Figure 9.4: Wealth allocation statement

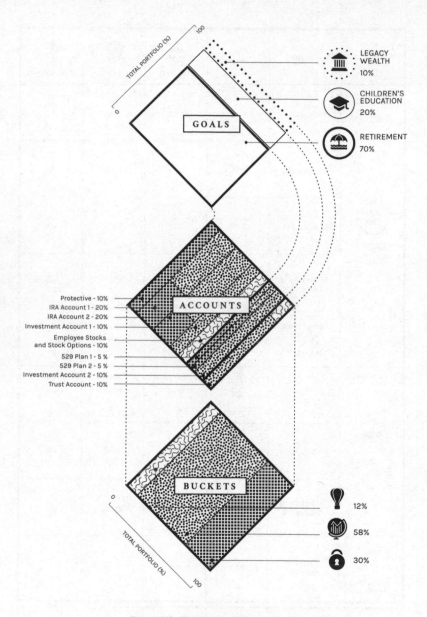

TOTAL PORTFOLIO (%)

GOALS

LEGACY WEALTH
10%

CHILDREN'S EDUCATION
20%

RETIREMENT
70%

Protective - 10%
IRA Account 1 - 20%
IRA Account 2 - 20%
Investment Account 1 - 10%
Employee Stocks and Stock Options - 10%
529 Plan 1 - 5 %
529 Plan 2 - 5 %
Investment Account 2 - 10%
Trust Account - 10%

ACCOUNTS

BUCKETS

TOTAL PORTFOLIO (%)

12%

58%

30%

Figure 9.5: Wealth allocation overview

If you conclude that your ability and your desire to bear risk are at odds, then you might wish to err on the side of a more moderate risk exposure. The financial and psychological dimensions of risk tolerance are illustrated in Figure 9.6. For simplicity, the diagram assumes just three allocations, defined as *conservative*, *moderate*, and *aggressive*.

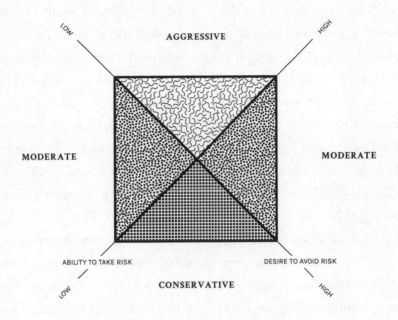

Figure 9.6: Interpreting your risk tolerance

Your ability to bear risk isn't the only relevant factor. Consider time horizon. One of the biggest fallacies about markets is that your investment risk decreases as your time horizon increases. In truth, as discussed in Chapter 3, markets can and do go out of existence. Thus the uncertainty of investment outcomes *usually increases with time.* To be sure, a longer time horizon can help cushion the impact of any adjustments you might need to make to your lifestyle, goals, investment strategy, or savings behavior. If you do not need your money for a long time, and can make adjustments to your lifestyle along the way, then you may indeed be able to take more risk. However, when faced with current or future cash shortfalls, especially with regard to retirement savings, the common trope—simply allocate more money to equities—rests on faulty logic and is certainly no panacea for reversing negative cash flow.

Another key factor is the ratio of your current wealth to the amount of money you need to sustain your lifestyle. An oft-repeated proverb holds that "wealth can be measured in years," a sentiment that refers to the wisdom and experience that we accumulate over a lifetime. The wealth management corollary is to estimate your current net worth in terms of the number of years of spending available to you. That number compared to your life expectancy plus, say, ten additional years for good measure, should give you a quick back-of-the-envelope figure that tells you whether you are on track.

Your earning potential is a final consideration that must be factored into the risk tolerance equation. Individuals in professions such as medicine, engineering, law, and corporate management have significant human capital that is transformed into substantial financial capital over a working lifetime. At early to mid-stages of their careers, these professionals tend to be income rich but asset poor in relation to other professions that do not require such extensive education and training. If this scenario describes your present situation, you should consider your investment in education and professional training to be a part of your overall safety portfolio. This categorization allows you to place more of your current investments in your market and aspirational portfolios than the average investor. Such reasoning may also guide you to buy a house or office earlier in your professional life, a step that is certainly justifiable, assuming that it helps build your career by establishing you in the community where you work.

Conversely, if you are approaching retirement and have mostly depleted your earnings potential, you should consider investing in the more risky aspirational bucket only if you are already affluent, have a strong desire to substantially increase your current net worth, and are willing to risk capital in order to do so. On the plus side, individuals in the pre-retirement phase possess considerable experience and extensive contacts. Many should (and often do) remain employed through consulting and other independent activities even after retirement. Pursuing compensated work can keep you active, help sustain your savings, and potentially enable you to delay spending down your assets.

Once you've determined that your wealth level is sufficient—that is, you've confirmed that you have the necessary margin of safety built into your safety portfolio—the obvious question is whether you want to take more risk, or reduce your risk to help ensure that you do not erode your safety net. Most investors instinctively feel that reducing risk is the best answer. Unfortunately, though, this answer is not completely satisfying. That's because portfolios invested and periodically rebalanced in accordance with the three-bucket Wealth Allocation Framework may well provide more safety over the long term than excessively "safe" portfolios that are concentrated in the safety bucket. The reason: demanding excessive safety over long periods creates its own risks, since it is not in the nature of the world to provide safety at a low cost. Consider, for example, the counter-party risk of your insurance provider, or the high fees and complexity of investments that aim to deliver safety, even when markets are uncertain. Managers of these investments must also undertake expensive, active hedging strategies to mitigate market volatility. Thus, it is always important to distinguish between market volatility and the risk of permanent loss of capital.

STEP 5: IMPLEMENT ASSET ALLOCATION AND
PORTFOLIO DIVERSIFICATION

Once you are satisfied that your risk allocation expresses properly how much risk you can (and should) comfortably take, it's time to allocate your assets prudently across the safety, market, and aspirational portfolios, and then to diversify within each.

Just as the goals of each risk bucket are different, so, too, are the securities that you will hold within them, as well as the way each portfolio is constructed. For example, you can put together your safety portfolio by considering your various risk factors and allocating resources to mitigate them. This can range from a reasonable down payment on a home along with a thirty-year mortgage, to buying enough term life insurance to protect your family in case of an unfortunate event.

The allocation of capital to mitigate each risk in the safety bucket can be quite uneven. In the market bucket the goal is achieving market return through diversification. A great deal has been written about the best way to construct a market portfolio, which is the subject of the next chapter. Finally, capital allocated to the aspirational bucket is often focused on one principal venture.

STEP 6: ANALYZE AND STRESS TEST

This step is crucial: ensuring that your risk allocation and supporting portfolio strategy are shockproof. A standard Monte Carlo scenario analysis tool such as those employed by many financial advisors will provide you with the probability of achieving your goals. You want to be on track to reaching your essential goals with at least 80 percent probability, perhaps closer to 95 percent or 100 percent if you can. However, the incremental cost of certainty can get very expensive over the long term and becomes a matter to work out with your advisor.

To be sure, there are many more risks than those measured by the standard deviation of a normal distribution, as we have seen. It is thus important to test your portfolio against those seemingly "rare" market disruptions that seem to occur with alarming frequency.

Market Meltdown Test: This is the simplest, of course. Imagine you are in a situation where the market has fallen by 50 percent and your aspirational assets are worth zero. Your safety portfolio may also have taken a hit, with your home value down 20 percent. What impact does this situation have on your essential goals and meeting your family's basic needs? If the results are catastrophic or unimaginable, you definitely need to rethink your current portfolio: such crashes can and have occurred throughout history, especially in the span of a human lifetime.

You might also wish to test your strategy against a few other extreme events such as the following:

Loss of Employment Test: You lose your employment, your income ceases while your cash outflows remain constant, and the markets drop 50 percent. Would you still be able to protect your minimum wealth level? For how long? Could you keep key assets like your home or would you be forced to sell them at fire-sale prices?

Sustainability Test: For how long can your core financial assets (excluding personal assets like a home or car, as well as your aspirational investments) sustain your lifestyle?

Aspirational Goals Test: Looking exclusively at your aspirational goals, are you satisfied that there is a reasonable chance of achieving some of them? If not, would you be willing to take more risk, without endangering your essential goals? Would you be willing, instead, to adjust your aspirational goals?

Sources of Return Test: For each asset and cash inflow, identify the sources of return. What do they rely on and how certain are they?

Difficult to Quantify Risks Test: Define your hard-to-quantify risks. Could the cash flows change? Could your family situation change? What about a once-in-a-century earthquake or hurricane? Under what circumstances might there be no buyers when you wish to sell? What would happen if [. . .]?

Tests such as these are often hard to quantify, so there is a tendency to skip them or at least not to review them regularly. But in a really challenging situation, the soundness of this thinking will be critical to the survival of your wealth management strategy and offers the added insurance that your essential goals will be able to withstand a shock to the system.

STEP 7: REVIEW AND REBALANCE

On an annual basis, it's important to track how you are doing and to reassess your goals and risk allocation throughout market cycles and in the context of your current life stage. Simply put, you must evaluate how much security you need (safety portfolio) versus capital you are willing to risk losing completely (aspirational portfolio), and then put the rest in a diversified market portfolio.

Wealth is not an absolute number per se. Rather, wealth can and should be defined relative to your needs—for example, as the number of years of current spending you have invested in your safety and market portfolios. The definition of a "minimum" wealth level is important and deserves monitoring over time. After all, your risk-taking ability and preferences will change over time, as you increase or decrease your wealth relative to your basic needs. Figure 9.7 offers a visual example of a changing risk profile and risk allocation, based on wealth relative to a previously identified minimum level.

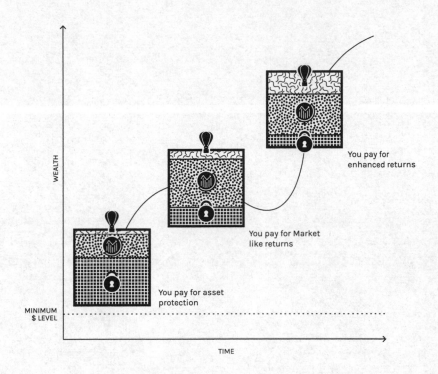

Figure 9.7: Dynamic nature of risk allocation over time

Sticking to the above-outlined seven-step process in a disciplined fashion through all kinds of market cycles—from boring markets to market bubbles and crashes—is likely to yield better results than most active managers can deliver. More important, these steps are your road map for achieving life goals in a world where money and markets are a necessary input but not an end unto themselves.

10

Owning the World

It's no coincidence that the centerpiece of the Wealth Allocation Framework is the market portfolio. The "market," as we have seen in the earlier chapters, represents the aggregate wisdom of the crowd as well as the foolishness of the masses. It is the most efficient way an individual investor can participate in the growth and innovation of society, as it evolves over time. There is, however, one important caveat: groupthink amplifies the foolishness. Cooler heads may prevail over the long term, but in the short term market investors must be prepared for a volatile ride. A well-diversified market portfolio will deliver market return with market risk, yet it does so on its own terms, unaware and uncaring of your needs and aspirations. Whether markets are efficient or not, the evidence suggests that most investors would be hard-pressed to do better.

Most of your assets should be held in your market portfolio, unless there is a compelling reason to put them elsewhere. Seeking safety (not just of principal but also for peace of mind) is one such valid reason, and assets allocated to the safety bucket provide just that, at least in the short term. But this deviation from your allocation to the market comes at a price: the loss of market return. Therefore, the amount you allocate to your safety portfolio must be determined with great care. While you may enjoy the benefits of safety in the short term, the price you pay over the long term is measured in loss of market return and a higher hurdle to cross when it comes to keeping up with the cost of living.

This point is intuitively obvious when you consider the role of cash in your portfolio. Cash is, simultaneously, an angel of safety in the short term but a devil that drags down your returns in the long term. Similarly, assets held in your aspirational portfolio also come at a steep price: the danger of catastrophic loss. Therefore, as argued in previous chapters, you cannot depend on your aspirational assets for your essential goals.

This brings us to the all-important question of how exactly you should construct your market portfolio. Put another way: What is the optimal way to capture returns and manage risk while investing in the financial markets?

To answer this question, let's revisit the principles of modern portfolio theory. The paper that laid the foundations for the theory, became an investment classic, and earned a Nobel Prize for its creator, Harry Markowitz, happened almost by chance. When Markowitz was a young graduate student in the early 1950s casting about for a dissertation topic, his focus was not on finance but rather on the then-burgeoning discipline of optimization known as linear programming. Waiting in the anteroom to meet with his University of Chicago advisor, Markowitz began a conversation with another individual who was also there waiting—a stockbroker. The man suggested Markowitz figure out how to maximize return in the stock market. The young graduate student took the suggestion seriously and, as they say, the rest is history. Efficient market theorists, not without some humor and irony, summarize this exchange as "the best tip from a stockbroker in the history of financial markets."

In his novel framework, Markowitz shifted the focus from maximizing return from the stock market to maximizing return for a given level of risk taken on by an investor. For the definition of the risk of a security or a portfolio, Markowitz focused on volatility, that is, the variability of returns, and borrowed directly from the field of statistics: he chose standard deviation (the square root of the variance of returns) as his measure of choice. A safe security would give you a fixed return with little risk or variability. A risky security would promise a higher return, but one that is less certain and accompanied by higher volatility. An investor would thus have to accept more uncertainty in the pursuit of higher returns. Therefore, in an efficient market, risk (represented by volatility) and expected return are directly related. Notice that, in this discussion, the distinction between uncertainty and volatility is lost. The need to preserve that distinction, as we have discussed in earlier chapters, is indeed one of the reasons for the creation of the Wealth Allocation Framework.

Markowitz also argued that, if you wanted to maximize return for an acceptable level of volatility (as determined by the investor), you could do better than just pick one stock that meets that risk-return profile. Instead, a superior, or more "efficient," approach is to combine different securities or asset classes, such as stocks and bonds, to collectively provide a risk-return profile desired by the investor. This is the principle of diversification. The degree of market exposure is often referred to by professionals as the "beta" of a portfolio, with a beta of 1 meaning that a portfolio will move up and down in tandem, and with the same percentage of gains and losses, as the equity market.

In theory, at least, a diversified portfolio always does better than a single stock with the same risk profile. Intuitively (and mathematically), portfolio returns are more stable and the portfolio itself is perhaps less risky if all of its investments are not perfectly correlated, meaning that they do not all lose value at the same time. A simple example: while stocks are falling, bonds may hold their value, thus reducing the magnitude of the "drawdown," or decline, of the overall portfolio.

Within the parameters of his framework, Markowitz provided an algorithm to maximally (or "efficiently") reduce risk, what investment professionals today call "mean-variance optimization." Choosing the right combination of securities and appropriately sizing these positions relative to each other, based on the risk and correlation characteristics of each investment, would enable investors to reduce the volatility of their portfolios and make some of the risk disappear, without sacrificing returns.

Markowitz called the risk that investors could eliminate through diversification "idiosyncratic risk," and argued that the market would not pay them for it. Of course, active managers do choose to take on some idiosyncratic risk, and the ensuing excess return (positive or negative) is known as alpha.

This stands in contrast to what Markowitz called systematic (market) risk, which investors do get paid to take on because it cannot be eliminated. Thus investments that are not perfectly correlated to each other, Markowitz found, can be judiciously combined to eliminate idiosyncratic risk. Markowitz called these optimized portfolios "efficient." These optimized portfolios lie on what he called the "efficient frontier," as illustrated in Figure 10.1.

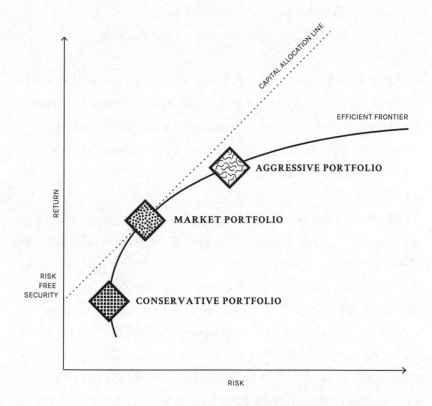

Figure 10.1: The Markowitz "efficient frontier"

Of course, the theory of diversification has been widely recognized and embraced for centuries, as captured in the familiar
admonition "Don't put all your eggs in one basket." In *The Rise and
Decline of the Medici Bank: 1397–1494*, author Raymond de Roover
points out that medieval merchant-adventurers sought protection
from high risks by carefully distributing their investments among
many different ventures. This policy was clearly expressed by Antonio in Shakespeare's *Merchant of Venice*:

My ventures are not in one bottom trusted,
Nor to one place; nor is my whole estate

Upon the fortune of this present year;

Therefore my merchandise makes me not sad.

Antonio may have been a fictional character, but Shakespeare's dialogue captures the essence of diversification, not just with regard to shipping vessels but also to geographical exposure and time. Of course, diversification isn't that easy in practice, and Antonio's exposure to a single industry, shipping, nearly led to the loss of his entire fortune.

These days the Markowitz framework is most often applied to determine an optimal portfolio composed of stocks, bonds, and cash. When you talk to your financial advisor, he or she will likely suggest one of the standard portfolios that lie on the "efficient frontier," after determining your risk profile. At the most basic level, what you need to decide is how much exposure you would like to take to the equity market, and then put the rest in bonds and cash. This key step is known today simply as asset allocation. At greater degrees of sophistication, advisors may discuss other ways of gaining exposure to sources of return, such as credit, and add other asset classes such as corporate bonds, high-yield debt, and so on (see Figure 10.2).

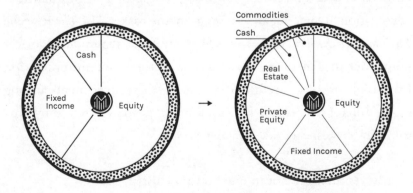

Figure 10.2: Simple vs. complex asset allocation models

Implementing a diversified asset allocation strategy may seem like a logical and simple procedure. Yet one could reasonably argue, as we have seen, that the elimination of what Markowitz called idiosyncratic risk (the kind of risk that can be diversified away) seems like a suboptimal strategy, if you believe in the power of active investment management.

Do you recall the almost surrealistic debate, described in Chapter 1, about whether money managers with sophisticated investment teams and ultra-fast computers could outperform dart throwers, especially after fees? Depending on your assessment of the skill of active money managers, there are essentially two divergent paths of implementation for the market portfolio: active or passive management. You can also choose to combine them.

Those who do not believe in active management should consider indexing. An inexpensive, market-weighted world equity index combined with a US or global bond index creates in one simple swoop a well-diversified, low-cost market portfolio. Additional work would be required to determine your recommended asset allocation, that is, what percentage of your portfolio should be in the equity index and how much should be allocated to the bond index. A well-established starting point is 60 percent in equities and 40 percent in bonds. Further, since you cannot time the market, you may want to average into the market over a period of time.

This simple construction ensures that you are well diversified and invested in the growth of the world. With periodic rebalancing and some year-end tax-loss harvesting you are done. Over the long term, if you are patient and disciplined with this strategy, your market portfolio will probably beat a majority of active money managers.

At this point, you might be asking yourself: "Wasn't the central argument of this book that you should invest to achieve your goals, not beat a market benchmark?" The answer is an unqualified yes. Recall that attempting to beat the market *in the context of your total portfolio* is a fool's errand. As we have seen, even by consistently outperforming the market, it is improbable to meaningfully move up the wealth spectrum on the strength of portfolio returns alone. Nonetheless, in the context of your market portfolio, *it is entirely appropriate to aim for outperformance from asset allocation, manager selection, and security selection.* It is within your market portfolio alone, therefore, that the active versus passive debate is no longer a false choice. Striving to beat a market index is an appropriate market portfolio–focused goal. Other appropriate goals might be: an absolute rate of return, or a more sophisticated risk-adjusted return target (such as the Sharpe ratio), or a goal of earning an incremental rate of return above inflation (a particularly appropriate goal for foundations and endowments).

The ongoing debate about the relative merits of active versus passive investment management plays out in other important ways. One fundamental and controversial framing of this issue centers on the relative importance, in driving portfolio returns, of asset allocation decisions versus the selection of individual securities. In a groundbreaking 1986 paper that examined the performance of ninety-one large US pension plans over a ten-year period (1974–1983), authors Gary Brinson, L. Randolph Hood, and Gilbert Beebower found that "investment policy (asset allocation) dominates investment strategy (market timing and security selection), explaining on average 93.6 percent of the variation in total plan return." These astounding findings, published in the influential *Financial Analysts Journal*, led professional investors, financial advisors, and investment committees to conclude that their time was best spent determining a target asset allocation for their institutions and clients, not picking stocks or managers.

As a result of this influential paper, many investment committees now consider determining an appropriate target asset allocation for their institution the cornerstone of their fiduciary responsibility. The target asset allocation in an investment policy statement is usually referred to simply as "the policy portfolio."

The idea that asset allocation reigns supreme over security selection is a subject of ongoing debate. Still, two key takeaways are clear:

- If your managers do not take big bets, then the alpha generated by your portfolio will be small and the return from market exposure (beta) will dominate. In addition, your portfolio's monthly performance will be highly correlated to the performance of your benchmark.
- If you want alpha, you will need to find a few very good managers and allow them the freedom to take concentrated, contrarian bets. Conversely, if you hold a large number of managers with similar strategies or constrain them on how much risk they can take, then your performance will approach that of the benchmark. Since active management is a zero-sum game, the active bets made by managers in aggregate tend to cancel each other out.

The upshot? A diversified portfolio delivers primarily the market return. *Therefore, in any given year, small tactical bets, made by either overweighting or underweighting a particular asset class or allocation to a specific investment manager, will not make much of a difference in your total return.* In this sense, the authors of the famous 1986 paper were probably right: in the long run, for the typical investor, the decisions you make about your strategic asset allocation will largely determine your total return, which will be close to what the market would have delivered with similar exposures.

The flip side of this observation is that, to deliver substantial alpha, investors must be willing to be strong contrarians and let their managers move boldly into investing strategies that most others (at that time) would not touch, or change the asset allocation target dynamically to dramatically overweight asset classes that seem to be undervalued. This type of higher-risk, active investing requires courage, great skill, experience, and some measure of luck. Not surprisingly, most institutions and investment committees are reluctant to put themselves on the line by providing that much freedom. Most active managers are thus relegated to making small bets around their benchmark to recover their fees and add some value.

There is considerable evidence, for example, that after periods when managers outperform—most often when they are first starting out and have only a small amount of capital to deploy—risk aversion takes hold, and they either consciously or subconsciously begin to hug their underlying benchmarks. This behavior allows managers to outperform relative to their benchmarks on an inception-to-date basis and preserve their franchises and reputations, even as they struggle to provide alpha on an ever-growing asset base.

Chasing yesterday's top managers, solely on the basis of their historical outperformance, is therefore not a sustainable investment strategy.

A recent study by asset management firm Vanguard quantifies the consequences of this behavior. In the fifteen years through 2010, only 111 of 263, or 42 percent, of actively managed domestic large-capitalization blend stock funds beat the Standard & Poor's 500 index. But even that lackluster number does not include the more than 200 "dead funds" (either closed or merged out of existence, presumably for lousy early performance) that didn't survive the full period analyzed. When the researchers accounted for these "dead funds," they found that only 23 percent of the active fund universe (111 out of 476 funds) managed to both endure and establish a decade-and-a-half track record of outperformance.

The market portfolio is designed to support your standard of living, not shoot the lights out. Aiming for a well-diversified portfolio (active or passive), with a sharp eye to performance after fees and taxes, is likely the surest path to sustainable returns.

So, if asset allocation is the key to successfully investing your market portfolio, and you are comfortable with getting a return closely correlated to what the market provides, what is the right way to go about it? Your diversification strategy need not be overly complex. A single broad index, three to five active managers, or thirty or so carefully picked securities, each with different strategies or market exposures, is all you need to capture the benefits of diversification for each asset class.

Indeed, naive diversification into expensive and illiquid asset classes can be costly. Asset classes such as hedge funds, venture capital, "frontier" markets, reinsurance strategies, pharmaceutical royalties, or even timber-producing land may seem to provide diversification to the standard mix of equities and bonds, but in practice they offer as many ways to destroy wealth as to build it. Extreme caution is required when pursuing asset classes or investment strategies that are neither widely accepted nor readily understood. If you have access to a strong due-diligence process and a good investment team that can find high-quality managers, then combining them with a disciplined investment process may indeed add considerable value over time, thanks to the power of compounding. That is, in effect, the Yale Endowment model.

One option for your market portfolio is to simply avoid the allure of exotic, hard-to-access asset classes altogether and to hold a diversified portfolio similar or even identical to a market-weighted benchmark. This approach, drawing on the "wisdom of crowds," is based on the assumption that the aggregate estimate of all investors with regard to where to invest is probably better than your own estimate, unless, of course, you are a sophisticated investor or have access to reliable advice in these areas.

Numerous empirical studies have indeed demonstrated that the wisdom of crowds trumps individual estimates in a variety of contexts. However, as writer James Surowiecki highlights in his well-known book on the subject, aptly entitled *The Wisdom of Crowds*, a group's estimate trumps individual estimates only when participants make their own decisions (or guesses) and are not influenced by fellow participants—and when individual results are then aggregated and averaged.

This is best demonstrated by the famous jelly bean experiment, in which a random crowd estimates the number of jelly beans in a jar. The mathematical average of all guesses is usually better than 80 percent of the individual guesses. The reason is that people make a variety of errors, but if you can get a large enough crowd, the errors they make often cancel each other out (overestimates cancel out underestimates, for example). If you have roughly an equal number of over- and underestimators, the average cancels out these errors to provide a surprisingly accurate answer.

Unfortunately, the opposite can be true in financial markets, where participants often abandon independent thinking and copy each other by chasing last year's hot returns. Such "groupthink" is what often leads to bubbles and market crashes.

The upshot is that it is not sufficient just to invest in a diversified market portfolio. One must be able to withstand the volatility that comes from holding a portfolio whose valuation is at the mercy of the crowds (recalling that, at least historically, one has been paid well to stay the course even in the face of a severe market correction). Further, during the ups and downs of market bubbles and crashes, it is useful to remember the distinction between permanent loss of capital and market or portfolio volatility. True diversification greatly reduces the probability of permanent loss of capital. The broad market usually recovers, but we do not know in advance how long it will take to do so: days, months, or years. Therefore it is essential to get the relative amounts in the safety bucket and market bucket right, in order to always be able to meet essential needs. An appropriately sized safety bucket will allow you to leave the investments in the market bucket alone, especially when they are down.

In fact, even in the absence of major bubbles, markets typically experience a strong rotation, in which different asset classes outperform and under-perform as the business cycle unfolds, as illustrated in Figure 10.3.

Figure 10.3: Asset class returns across business cycles and time

This phenomenon of sector rotation underscores the importance of another important action that holders of a market portfolio should adopt: rebalancing.

As assets appreciate over time and become overweighted, disciplined rebalancing forces you to sell them and buy those assets that are undervalued. Although you will almost certainly sell too early or buy too soon, *over the course of a market cycle you will end up selling high and buying low.* At the very least you won't get sucked into the return-chasing sentiment that drives most individual investors to buy high and sell low, as illustrated in Figure 10.4.

Rebalancing your assets is therefore a robust and disciplined way of introducing a value-based approach with only minor transaction costs, which in turn can be lowered through tax-aware strategies. To get started on the road to tax-aware investing, it is useful to think of some important ways to minimize tax impact. First, take advantage of tax-deferred accounts by fully funding a tax-deferred retirement account—such as a 401(k)—which may also be accompanied by an employer match, and by funding tax-deferred educational accounts, such as a 529 plan, for your children or grandchildren. Specific tax-advantaged securities such as municipal bonds make sense, especially if you are in a high tax bracket. You would normally avoid putting them in your tax-deferred retirement account, which would be a natural place for your high-yield investments. Before the end of each calendar year, it would be a good idea to rebalance your asset allocation with an eye to net gains and losses. These are general rules and there are many more, which are best implemented in consultation with an expert, such as your financial advisor and your accountant. In this way, tax-aware rebalancing is a valuable complement to your diversification strategy.

One way to improve the chances of sticking to a sensible rebalancing strategy is to automate the process and to create

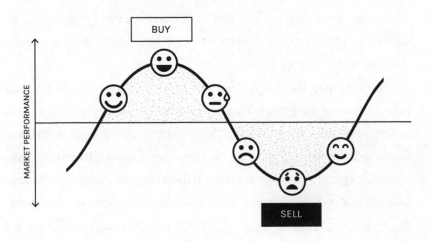

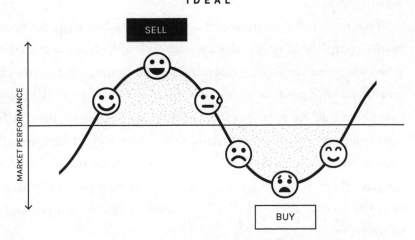

Figure 10.4: Emotion-driven investing vs regular rebalancing (ideal)

predetermined timetables for other important reevaluations. As discussed earlier, the end of the fiscal or calendar year is a natural milestone for tax-aware rebalancing. In fact, if you take advantage of incoming and outgoing cash flows as opportunities to also rebalance your portfolio, pulling out cash from overweighted assets or adding to underweighted assets, then you can considerably reduce the long-term cost of rebalancing.

So there you have it: investing in the market is about tapping into drivers of return and managing risk. In many cases there is not much you can do about the market's overall performance. But a sensible strategy, based on reasonable costs, diversification, asset allocation, and tax-aware rebalancing, can help you maintain your standard of living and should enable your market portfolio to fulfill its objectives. In return, you can expect to earn the market return for market volatility. Some investors can do better and will beat the market. However, as we have seen, this will not lead to the kind of wealth creation that propels mobility up the wealth spectrum.

That's not to say that a smart and disciplined strategy for your market portfolio won't make a measurable difference, especially when executed well over a sustained period of time, in how much wealth you accumulate or are able to spend each year. Whether you choose active management or indexing (or both), these different approaches to constructing your market portfolio are all reasonable choices to consider, as you explore what strategy works for you. Bear in mind, though, that it is far easier to do damage here than to "beat the market." "First do no harm" is a principle to invest by.

Some investors may find this conclusion unsatisfying and feel compelled to ask, "What am I missing?" What about those outsized market returns, the astounding wealth created by legendary investors such as Warren Buffett, or the track record of consistent investing success notched by major university endowments such as Yale's? These strategies, in fact, serve as a case study in how the Wealth Allocation Framework can be applied to sophisticated investment strategies, the subject of our next chapter.

ASPIRE!

Do Not Try This at Home

The practice of investing has had its share of fads and fashions. For sophisticated, wealthy investors, two approaches in particular have achieved legendary status, and for good reason.

The first is the strategy pioneered by the investment offices of two famous Ivy League universities, Yale and Harvard, for their endowments. Their strategies deployed so-called alternative investments, such as hedge funds and private equity, to help fuel impressive, multi-decade-long track records of exceptional investment returns. Indeed, few can lay claim to such amazing results. David Swensen, chief investment officer of the Yale endowment, has stewarded a sixteen-fold growth in the value of Yale's portfolio since taking the helm in 1985; and Jack Meyer, who steered Harvard's endowment from 1990 to 2005, delivered average annual returns of 15.9 percent during his tenure. The runaway success of Yale and Harvard has not gone unnoticed by the investment world, which now refers to this style of investing as the "Endowment model."

The second approach was pioneered by a man whose very name has become a brand unto itself: value investor Warren

Buffett, the "Oracle of Omaha," who has piloted his publicly traded investment vehicle, Berkshire Hathaway, to stunning success, outperforming the S&P 500 index, including dividends, by an annualized 9.9 percentage points from the beginning of 1965 through the end of 2013.

What, then, explains the astonishingly anomalous returns from these two investing approaches? An entire ecosystem of academics, advisors, and consultants has set about to answer this question. It is indeed an important one. Financial institutions and high-net-worth individuals alike have tried to copy this success, without fully understanding the nature of the underlying risk exposures.

For imitators of the Endowment model, in particular, that proved disastrous as the global financial crisis swept through markets in 2008. Although endowment portfolios appeared to be more diversified than conventional portfolios across both asset classes and investment strategies, they lost about as much as the global equity markets, with the best-performing endowments, those of Yale and Harvard, losing 27.3 percent and 24.6 percent, respectively, about on par with the 26.2 percent loss for the S&P 500 index that year. In effect, Endowment portfolios lost all of their diversification benefit and behaved as if they were 100 percent equity portfolios at precisely the worst time: during a market crash.

The pain did not end there. Portfolios built to mimic the Endowment model were underweighted in conventional bonds and had substantial capital commitments to private equity firms. These capital commitments were essentially promissory notes to private equity management companies (which were on the hunt for firms to take over) and could be called in at a moment's notice. Not meeting these capital calls could have led to a contractual default, thus causing the entire investment in that fund to be written off. Faced with a liquidity crisis, and unwilling to sell parts of their endowment at rock-bottom prices, Harvard canceled several major initiatives, and both institutions turned to the bond markets to raise capital. Fortunately for them, and despite the uncertainty of the times, both Yale and Harvard got a good reception from the fixed-income investors. Many other institutions were not so lucky, as they arrived at the investment party late but stayed just long enough to experience the crash, without having enjoyed the early gains.

For sophisticated investors seeking to emulate the Ivy endowments or to unlock the secrets to Warren Buffett's moneymaking prowess, it is imperative to understand the nature of these respective strategies, especially the potential risks. Peering into these strategies through the lens of the Wealth Allocation Framework yields some eye-opening insights that can help contextualize both the risk and the opportunity of these styles of investing, and the practicality of pursuing them.

The conclusions, as we shall see, are surprising. The Endowment model purports to be diversified, but from the point of view of the Wealth Allocation Framework it is actually concentrated in the market portfolio. Implementing the model involves risk-return trade-offs, as well as practical challenges, that may not be well recognized by many investors. Conversely, the conventional wisdom about Warren Buffett is that he concentrates his bets in just a few holdings. Buffett himself has said that "diversification is only required when investors do not know what they are doing (but still require exposure to the equity market)." But it turns out that Buffett's magic can in large part be explained by a novel approach to *risk allocation* that is, in reality, quite diversified.

THE ENDOWMENT MODEL

Let us begin our analysis with the Endowment model. The investment returns from the two leading institutional practitioners have been nothing short of stunning. In the tumultuous decade from July 1, 2000, to June 30, 2009, the S&P 500 index lost an average of 2.22 percent each year and a traditional portfolio with an allocation of 60 percent to stocks and 40 percent to bonds gained a meager 1.33 percent each year. During the same time period, Yale's endowment delivered an annualized return of 11.8 percent. Yale's performance was also far superior to the mean performance of a broad range of university endowments (see Figure 11.1), even after including the effects of the crash of 2008.

Over the past decade, many boutique outsourced "CIO" (chief investment officer) businesses were created with the value proposition of replicating the Endowment model for wealthy families, family offices, and small and midsize endowments.

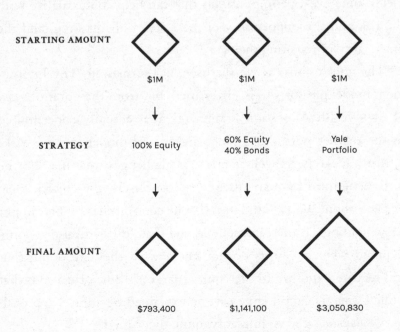

Figure 11.1: Performance of Yale's endowment (2000–2009)

So what exactly is the Endowment model? David Swensen's explanation of the endowment model, as outlined in his masterly book *Pioneering Portfolio Management*, emphasizes three key themes: a disciplined and well-thought-out investment process; "insightful implementation," with an emphasis on "avoiding or minimizing conflicts of interest that are present at every step of the investment process"; and "an understanding of what it takes to beat the market and the courage to stick to a contrarian but well-thought-out investing strategy."

Based on these three key principles, according to Swensen, the resulting portfolio:

- is equity heavy, to capture the equity risk premium and generate, on average, higher rates of return than bonds. This allows the portfolio to preserve, over the long term, its purchasing power with regard to inflation and also peer institutions.
- has a large component that is illiquid, to capture the illiquidity premium and thus take advantage of the very long-term investing horizon of the institution.
- is largely devoted to active investment management, with managers afforded considerable freedom to use their expertise to invest across a variety of strategies and asset classes in order to exploit inefficiencies in the markets.
- is characterized by investment terms and incentives that are structured to reduce or minimize conflicts of interest between investors and investment managers.
- allows managers wide freedom on investment strategies and implementation of their strategies through customized investment vehicles. This means that many of the underlying investments in the portfolio may *not be through public* stock, mutual funds, or index funds, but through partnerships such as hedge funds or private equity vehicles.

For convenience and scalability, financial institutions and high-net-worth investors that have tried to copy the Endowment model have lumped these nontraditional, illiquid strategies into a single sleeve commonly referred to as "alternative investments." As the name suggests, these investments are considered "alternatives" to allocations to traditional asset classes such as cash, fixed income, and equity, even though they are often initially carved out of the traditional equity allocation.

While the recommended asset allocation of a wealthy investor often includes an allocation to alternative investments, the Yale and Harvard asset allocations—that is, their "policy portfolios"—go much further, as illustrated in Figure 11.2.

So what went wrong with the Endowment model of investing in 2008? One way to answer this question is to assess the Endowment model through the lens of the Wealth Allocation Framework.

Over time, all of these institutions began to substitute some of their asset-liability matching bond investments (safety) with alternative investments (market), based on the (incorrect) argument that the diversified nature of these investments reduced the risk of the overall portfolio, thus necessitating a smaller allocation to safety assets such as bonds.

On the eve of the global financial crisis the endowment portfolios of both Yale and Harvard were overweight in the market portfolio, with little to no allocation to the safety and aspirational portfolios as shown in Figure 11.3. This may seem surprising, given that investments such as hedge funds and private equity, which make up the bulk of the portfolios, are generally perceived to be aimed at producing outsized, aspirational returns. But remember that aspirational investments require alpha associated with human capital, coupled with leverage and concentration, to create substantial impact. Yale's private equity and long-short and distressed hedge fund investments were made in a prudent and diversified

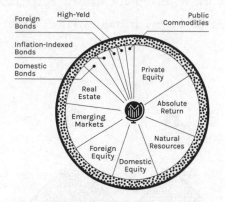

HARVARD
ENDOWMENT POLICY PORTFOLIO 2013

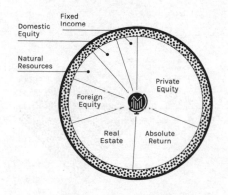

YALE
ENDOWMENT POLICY PORTFOLIO 2013

Figure 11.2: Harvard and Yale endowment policy portfolios

fashion, designed to tap into the superior investing skills of their investment managers and to provide marginally higher returns than the market. My placement of these investments in the market portfolio appears to be entirely consistent with Swensen's own writings on his investment strategy.

"Yale's portfolio is structured using a combination of academic theory and informed market judgment," Swensen writes. "The theoretical framework relies on the Mean-Variance analysis, an approach developed by Nobel laureates James Tobin and Harry Markowitz."

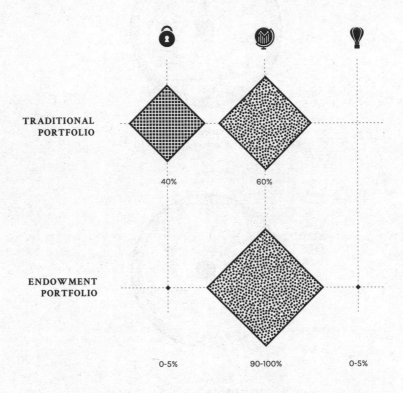

Figure 11.3: Risk allocation of traditional portfolios versus endowment model portfolios (estimated)

As noted in Chapter 8, when assessing where to place a security or investment within a *risk bucket*, you must consider both the risk and return profile of the investment *and* the purpose it serves in the portfolio. One of the central tenets of the Endowment model approach is an emphasis on equity exposure in order to take advantage of the "equity risk premium" (the excess return that investors demand in exchange for stock market risk).

Consider two specific equity-related investment strategies, long-short equity hedge funds and private equity, that came into the popular lexicon of high-net-worth investors due in large part to the success of the Endowment model. In the previous chapter we went over the important concepts of beta (return that comes from exposure to market risk) and alpha (return that comes from a manager's skills). The difference between a long-only strategy and a long/short strategy centers on the relative emphasis of market beta and manager alpha.

From the viewpoint of the Wealth Allocation Framework, it is clear that these strategies are not designed as safety assets or insurance, in which nearly all of the return is given up in exchange for risk mitigation. Nor are they sized and constructed in order to generate triple-digit returns and make a major impact on the institution's overall balance sheet. Instead, leverage and idiosyncratic risk are balanced with market exposures in an effort to earn a better risk-return profile than mainstream investing strategies. There is no single investment that will create significant "game-changing" aspirational wealth. The emphasis is on managing risk and *delivering a higher compounded rate of return over time that should result in significant wealth over the long haul.*

Endowment model investors enjoy other advantages. They can provide investment managers considerable discretion in how best to structure their investments, whether through private partnerships for hedge funds or private equity fund structures, and make long-term capital commitments—to venture capital, for instance—that, if successful, will return money over a period of five to fifteen years. Endowment model investors often have the clout to negotiate terms with managers and secure fee structures that involve profit sharing, thus creating a better alignment of interests.

The implementation hurdles are also quite substantial. One of the biggest risks is what professionals call "manager selection": the ability to pick top-performing managers. This access, incredibly hard to come by, is absolutely critical to the success of endowments like Yale and Harvard, given the dispersion of returns between the top-performing managers of illiquid strategies and the bottom-performing ones (see Figure 11.4).

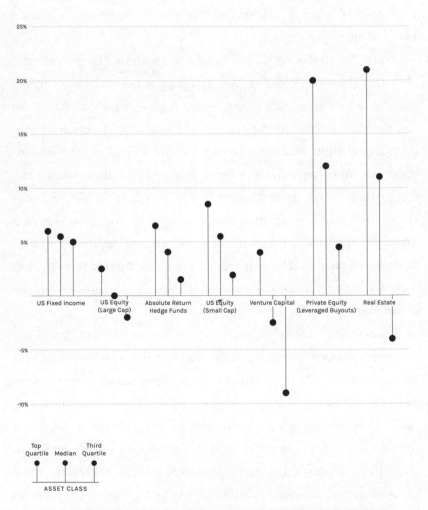

Figure 11.4: Dispersion of active manager returns (June 30, 2000–June 30, 2010)

Yale and Harvard, in particular, have carefully examined their competitive edge and reached similar conclusions: unlike most individual investors, they can take a very long-term view, put in place an excellent governance structure and investment process, fund the development of a first-rate team to expertly execute their investment process, and tap alumni worldwide to provide access to the top investment managers in the world.

Still, there are hidden potential risks to this strategy. To better understand them, let's complete the *risk allocation* picture of Yale's 2008 endowment portfolio by adding liabilities to our framework (Figure 11.5). Private equity and real estate commitments are not outstanding loans but rather promissory notes for a line of credit to be invested in illiquid and distressed investments that, when restructured and liquidated at an opportune time, should provide a superior rate of return. A severe market crash creates a myriad of opportunities for a sophisticated investor with ready access to capital. Thus, if these commitments were called in rapidly, the key question was: How would the endowment meet its commitments?

This is where a prior simple scenario analysis would have proved illuminating. In the Endowment model, existing private equity and real estate investments pay distributions that can fund future commitments. It is not unlike having a basket of high dividend–paying stocks and committing to invest in future ventures by assuming that you will fund them through the stock dividends. If you match your future commitments carefully with your anticipated dividends, all should go well. But in a major market dislocation or crash, things can go very wrong. Consider the impact. Assume that the Yale portfolio of 2008 declined by 25 percent. In that scenario, Yale's market portfolio would be worth $18 billion, of which only $9 billion is liquid. There is no asset/liability matching as with a pension fund,

	SAFETY	MARKET	ASPIRATIONAL
ASSETS	40%	60%	0%
BUDGETED 3 YEARS OF WITHDRAWALS FROM THE ENDOWMENT TO SUPPORT INSTITUTION (THE DRAW)	-15% (5% a year)		
TOTAL	25%	60%	0%

	SAFETY	MARKET	ASPIRATIONAL
ASSETS	0%	95% - 100%	0% - 5%
DRAW (3 YEARS)	-15%		
PRIVATE EQUITY & REAL ESTATE COMMITMENTS	33%		
TOTAL	-15% to -45%	95% - 100%	0% - 5%

Figure 11.5: Risk allocation of traditional 60/40 portfolio compared to the endowment model

and endowment portfolios have very little traditional fixed income and cash. From this liquid portion, Yale's endowment overseers would have to meet potential liabilities of $10 billion. Theoretically, the endowment has a serious liquidity issue. Thus, without a safety net, this strategy is a risky one.

In reality, there are many mitigating circumstances—for example, noting that its clients are in a liquidity crunch, the private equity managers might not call all of the capital due, thus reducing the draw. That is a tough assumption to make, for it pits the opportunity for the fund manager to make an outsized return in a currently distressed market against the desire for it to retain its large blue-chip clients for its future fund offerings. The endowment's parent institution could also leverage its credit rating to raise capital in the bond markets to cover shortfalls or it could tap alumni networks. Each alternative comes with its own set of costs.

In fairness, many of Yale's contingencies came through (as did Harvard's): private equity managers did not make devastating capital calls, belt-tightening helped reduce costs, capital projects were postponed, and bonds were issued. The bond market gave Yale a AAA rating. This proved that even at the height of the fiscal crisis, the public viewed providing a great education as a better business model than almost any other business in America.

Yet all of this came at a considerable human cost. The people laid off, in many cases, were not the highest-paid employees of these educational institutions but rather support staff (groundskeepers, janitors, secretaries), most of whom had meager savings and a very hard time finding other employment at the height of the recession. Yale itself did not emerge unscathed from the financial crisis, and its investment office shed its bulletproof (or should we say recession-proof) reputation, but the university did get to keep a good part of the amazing gains that it had built up earlier in the decade.

The implications for individual investors seeking to emulate Yale's approach are striking. We can see that, even though endowment portfolios appear to be fully diversified investment solutions, most implementations of the model are best understood as a form of "next generation," actively managed market portfolios. The Yale portfolio, over the years, had moved its (safety) bond portfolio into the market portfolio. In normal markets this next generation market portfolio seemed to be more diversified than just an equity portfolio. However, when the market crashed and all of the risky assets reacted to one factor—fear—the "stress beta" of the portfolio turned out to be about 1. The diversified endowment portfolio went down by about the same order of magnitude as the equity market.

Therefore, the Endowment model is, at best, an incomplete solution for individuals—regardless of their net worth. This is best seen by examining the endowment portfolio in the context of the Wealth Allocation Framework for a representative institution like Yale (see Figure 11.6).

Consider the long-term nature of Yale's overarching goal: to remain one of the world's top educational and research institutions for the next several hundred years. Achieving this goal requires maintaining basic standards, the campus, and so on, but also constantly investing in new areas, attracting top talent (students and faculty) from all over the world, maintaining the brand, and so forth. These goals require a tremendous degree of investing for the future, especially in areas that may or may not turn out to be useful. The "arms race," even among universities, is an expensive one!

In a 1997 interview, Yale law professor Henry Hansmann told the *New York Times* that "a stranger from Mars observing a large university like Yale or Harvard would see institutions whose

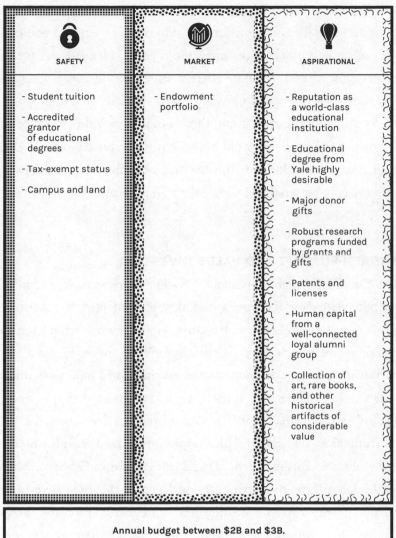

SAFETY	MARKET	ASPIRATIONAL
- Student tuition - Accredited grantor of educational degrees - Tax-exempt status - Campus and land	- Endowment portfolio	- Reputation as a world-class educational institution - Educational degree from Yale highly desirable - Major donor gifts - Robust research programs funded by grants and gifts - Patents and licenses - Human capital from a well-connected loyal alumni group - Collection of art, rare books, and other historical artifacts of considerable value

Annual budget between $2B and $3B.

Some of the expenses are essential; a large part falls in the important or aspirational category.

Figure 11.6: Risk allocation statement of an Ivy League endowment

business is to manage large pools of investment assets and that they run educational institutions on the side that can expand and contract to act as buffers for the investment pool." Hansmann's acerbic observation turned out to be correct, especially in 2008, when the investment fat tail ended up wagging the institutional dog.

As they found out in 2008, those envious of Yale's superior investment performance would have been well advised to study their own goals and risk-return profile before embarking on copying Yale's deeply original and well-executed investment strategy.

WARREN BUFFETT AND VALUE INVESTING

The Oracle of Omaha is without a doubt America's most recognized and adored investor. Known for his folksy, plain manner, the chairman, CEO, and top shareholder of Berkshire Hathaway has made a fortune disdaining the principles of diversification. Who are we to argue?

For many years the richest man in the world (and perennially near the top of the list), Buffett has a track record that is simply astonishing in terms of raw investment returns and longevity.

Buffett's value investing philosophy originated with his mentor and Columbia Business School professor Benjamin Graham, whose methodology was most famously outlined in the 1934 investment classic *Security Analysis*, coauthored with fellow professor David Dodd. This book, known today simply as "Graham and Dodd," remains the intellectual genesis of the value investing movement.

Writing in the fall 1984 issue of *Hermes*, the magazine of Columbia Business School, Buffett himself highlighted the superior performance of value investors: "I submit to you that there are ways of defining an origin other than geography. In addition to geographical origins, there can be what I call an intellectual origin. I think you will find that a disproportionate number of successful

coin-flippers in the investment world came from a very small intellectual village that could be called 'Graham–and-Doddsville.'
A concentration of winners that simply cannot be explained by
chance can be traced to this particular intellectual village."

Buffett went on to outline the amazing track records of nine of
Graham's former students, emphasizing the superiority of value investing when coupled with the qualities of intellect, character, and
temperament: "So these are nine records of 'coin-flippers' from
Graham-and-Doddsville. I haven't selected them with hindsight
from among thousands. It's not like I am reciting to you the names
of a bunch of lottery winners—people I had never heard of before
they won the lottery. I selected these men years ago based upon
their framework for investment decision-making. I knew what
they had been taught and additionally I had some personal knowledge of their intellect, character, and temperament."

And finally, debunking any connection between risk and
reward, contrary to Markowitz's framework, he writes: "It's very
important to understand that this group has assumed far less risk
than average; note their record in years when the general market
was weak. While they differ greatly in style, these investors are,
mentally, always buying the business, not buying the stock. A few of
them sometimes buy whole businesses. Far more often they simply
buy small pieces of businesses. Their attitude, whether buying all
or a tiny piece of a business, is the same. Some of them hold portfolios with dozens of stocks; others concentrate on a handful. But
all exploit the difference between the market price of a business
and its intrinsic value. . . . Today value investors may still vary in
their approaches, but they all have that one element in common:
they work to exploit the potentially lucrative disconnect between
the market price of a company, as reflected by its stock or sale price,
and the intrinsic value of the underlying business."

Buffett has made no secret of the additional factors that attract him to companies that fit this criteria: the quality of management, the replacement costs of the company or product, and deep "moats," or barriers, that prevent the competition from muscling in on market share or forcing down prices.

Still, value investing does not provide a complete explanation of Buffett's remarkable success. In fact, it is only part of the picture. Analyzing Berkshire Hathaway's operations through the lens of the Wealth Allocation Framework illustrates how Buffett makes use of safety and aspirational portfolios, in addition to the market portfolio. It also helps explain why he outperforms many of his peers, who focus on just that middle risk bucket.

To undertake such an analysis, it is important to first paint a picture of Berkshire's varied parts. The company is a conglomerate made up of many different businesses, from Borsheim's Fine Jewelry in Omaha, where Buffett and his company are based, to ketchup maker Heinz to Burlington Northern Santa Fe, which operates one of the largest rail networks in the United States.

One of the most important industries represented in the Berkshire portfolio is insurance, which Buffett himself describes as a "core operation." Why is insurance so crucial to Buffett's success?

In Berkshire Hathaway's 2013 Annual Report, Buffett provides the simple, compelling answer: "Property-casualty ('P/C') insurers receive premiums up front and pay claims later. In extreme cases, such as those arising from certain workers' compensation accidents, payments can stretch over decades. This collect-now, pay-later model leaves P/C companies holding large sums—money we call 'float'—that will eventually go to others. Meanwhile, insurers get to invest this float for their benefit."

Thus Buffett's magic isn't just limited to his selection of

well-run, profitable businesses held for the long term, based on the principles of value investing. It depends also on how he deploys the float earned by Berkshire's extraordinarily well-run insurance businesses, the most important of which are BH Reinsurance, General Re, and GEICO. Buffett redeploys these insurance proceeds (from the aspirational portfolio) into a market portfolio composed of diversified, profitable, well-run companies while holding considerable capital (as cash and short-term investments) in the safety portfolio and market portfolios, which provide both for a margin of safety and the ammunition for opportunistic investments. The *risk allocation* of Berkshire Hathaway is illustrated in Figure 11.7.

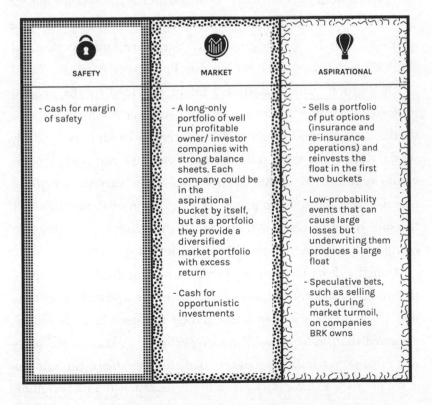

SAFETY

- Cash for margin of safety

MARKET

- A long-only portfolio of well run profitable owner/ investor companies with strong balance sheets. Each company could be in the aspirational bucket by itself, but as a portfolio they provide a diversified market portfolio with excess return

- Cash for opportunistic investments

ASPIRATIONAL

- Sells a portfolio of put options (insurance and re-insurance operations) and reinvests the float in the first two buckets

- Low-probability events that can cause large losses but underwriting them produces a large float

- Speculative bets, such as selling puts, during market turmoil, on companies BRK owns

Figure 11.7: Risk allocation for Berkshire Hathaway, Inc. (estimated by the author)

Buffett's liquid war chest represents a considerable sum: since the end of 2011, Berkshire's cash soared 30 percent, to more than $48 billion as of early 2014. Such vast sums enable Buffett to be "greedy when others are fearful," an advantage that he has exploited time and again to great profit. In 2008, for example, Buffett bought preferred shares and warrants on very generous terms in leading companies like General Electric and Goldman Sachs, when they urgently needed to shore up capital in the wake of the global financial crisis. The following year, in 2009, Berkshire made its then-largest-ever acquisition, the $26.7 billion purchase of Burlington Northern. Buffett has said that he aims to keep at least $20 billion in cash in reserve.

Over time, as Berkshire has become larger, it has become harder to find undervalued companies of the scale that would move the needle. Recently, for the first time, Berkshire under-performed the S&P 500 over a five-year period. The equity markets, fueled by the liquidity and inexpensive credit provided by the Federal Reserve, have had a strong post-2008 market rebound. In particular the S&P 500 returned 128 percent as of January 1, 2014, while, during the same time period, Berkshire Hathaway's book value increased by about 84 percent. Some shareholders have urged Berkshire to begin paying out a portion of Berkshire's vast treasure trove of cash in the form of dividends, something the company has not done since 1967 and Buffett opposes.

Buffett's short-term under-performance highlights an important insight about money management and the investment process: when a manager sticks to a disciplined framework, it should be expected that he or she will under-perform the market for periods of time. As Buffett's mentor, Benjamin Graham, himself put it, "The stock market is a voting machine rather than a weighing machine." His statement has been interpreted as emphasizing that in the short term the market is like a voting machine and rewards companies that are popular. But in the long run, the market is like a weighing machine: it assesses the true worth of the business. Over the long term, even after including Berkshire's recent five-year under-performance, the combination of genius and investing discipline has yielded for its shareholders roughly twice the return of the S&P 500.

Thus it probably doesn't pay for long-term investors to bet against Buffett, even (or especially) when he is suffering a rare bout of under-performance (relative to a sustained bull market). My analysis shows that the key ingredient in Buffett's recipe for success is a very sophisticated *risk allocation*, of which large amounts of cash are an essential ingredient. Investors should probably hesitate before asking for any of that cash back in the form of a dividend.

So what can we learn by studying the methodology of sophisticated investment strategies? For starters, beware the impulse to naively copy them. Not only are the strategies of David Swensen and Warren Buffett hard to replicate, but also the drivers of excess return often contain embedded risks that need to be carefully managed and that imitators rarely understand. The concentrated, value-based strategy of Berkshire Hathaway turns out to be surprisingly well diversified across all three risk buckets. Conversely, the Endowment model of investing, that at first glance seems to be a nice diversification of Markowitz's approach, turns out to be mostly concentrated in the market bucket, that is, a well-chosen but illiquid equity–heavy portfolio with no safety net. It's no wonder that Yale's endowment crashed in 2008 almost exactly in line with equity markets, leaving imitators and many universities and endowments in a precarious position. On the other hand, Berkshire Hathaway has managed to steer through many a market crisis over the decades, often shining during market downturns.

Perhaps the many imitators should heed the advice that David Swensen himself offers his fellow Yale alumni, who might be tempted to emulate his success: "Do not try this at home." After all, the Yale strategy is really only suitable for institutions with a variety of strong safety nets that exist outside of the investment portfolio, such as those that a leading university can access and that, alas, most individuals cannot. Similarly, retail investors seeking to replicate Warren Buffett's success would do well to pursue a more conventional route: buying Berkshire Hathaway's stock.

The Aspirational Society

The singular message of this book is that investing is not about the markets. Investing is about you. Your investment strategy can and must be designed to help you make progress toward the things that matter most. It should not be a blunt instrument of force, whose primary aim is to "beat the market." When executed properly, your investment strategy can fulfill your need for safety and give you a shot at your dreams and aspirations. Anything less would be, well, unsatisfying. After all, everyone wants to make a positive impact in his or her lifetime. It's not the money left when you die but how you made it, what it provided, and the legacy it has secured that truly matter.

My goal is to broaden the framework of investing. Building on the foundations of modern portfolio theory, the Wealth Allocation Framework described in these pages brings together insights about markets and manias, people and wealth, the rational mind and the behavioral complexities that influence our decision making. The principal insight of the Wealth Allocation Framework is that it refocuses the practice of investing on your goals and objectives. For this reason, the framework is a way to implement what I like to call *objective-driven investing.* It's a theory that is less about math equations and statistical formulae and more about what you hope to achieve in life.

Objective-driven investing captures two essential components of investing. A goals-driven framework should be defined by your "objectives," of course. But you also need an "objective" way of evaluating your progress—in other words, a reality check. Such a reality check should cover more than just your spending and savings patterns and whether they are aligned with your key goals such as building a financial safety net, maintaining your standard of living, and securing your retirement. This reality check should also include the understanding that goals such as safety and aspiration— the ability to preserve capital and the ability to earn outsized returns on capital—require very different risk-return profiles, portfolio construction, and portfolio sizing techniques, not to mention different benchmarks for evaluating performance objectively.

As I have argued in this book, a well-diversified market portfolio is important, but it is hardly sufficient. A safety portfolio is vital for navigating successfully through an uncertain and often volatile world, one where markets are unstable. Over the long term, investors with staying power can not only recoup losses but also position themselves, like Warren Buffett, to be greedy when others are fearful. We have also seen that, in today's society, wealth mobility comes not from a diversified market portfolio, at least not over a lifetime, but rather from the monetization of human capital or from successfully managing high-risk, high-potential-return assets or endeavors that are best held (and appropriately sized) in your aspirational portfolio.

We are lucky to be alive at such an amazing time in history. Our rapidly changing society is at the beginning of a third transformational wave that will profoundly affect human civilization.

The first big revolution was the agricultural revolution, which enabled mankind to sustain itself by understanding and harnessing the power of nature. Societies no longer had to wander from place to place in search of food. The stability that this engendered led to the further development and refinement of knowledge and eventually, after thousands of years, produced the scientific age, which in turn pointed the way to the Industrial Revolution and the mechanization of society. Instead of man versus nature, the dominant theme became man and machine, with the advent of steam power yielding massive productivity gains and the ability to transport manufactured goods across the globe in reliable and timely ways.

These transformations have come to us at a faster and faster pace. The Agricultural Revolution lasted thousands of years, the Industrial Revolution a mere two hundred before giving way to the Digital Revolution. In the information age, the focus now is the interaction between man and computer. This era is one of infinite possibility, perhaps best captured by the concept of "mass customization," an oxymoron of sorts, which is revolutionizing not only the consumer goods and entertainment sectors but also health care and medicine. Increased longevity is just one of the many important by-products of recent technological advancements that produce a double-edged sword: the blessing of a longer life, while at the same time the greatly increasing prospect of running out of money.

There are more transformational changes to come. Social networking curates information and knowledge and makes it instantly accessible to large segments of society. The advent of 3-D printing will democratize manufacturing. In turn, the term *manufacturing* no longer refers to merely making industrial machines or consumable goods but also encompasses bioengineering. This includes prosthetic limbs whose movements can be directly controlled by the human brain, as well as biological "spare parts," which range from heart valves to an entire bladder. Genetically modified seeds can and will be further customized to the local soil and climate.

All of these innovations force us to move faster just to stay relevant in society.

Investing in markets connects us to the great innovations of our age that contribute to the progress of our world. Even though great breakthroughs like these often lift all of society, they do so unevenly. In each area, the ability to access, understand, and curate large amounts of data to arrive at, manufacture, and deliver an optimal "product" for every individual will amplify the difference between the winner and the also-ran, in our winner-take-all society. Recall that even in one of the richest countries of the world, the United States of America, a third of the nation is already either insolvent or a single adverse event away from bankruptcy.

All of this raises the bar with respect to your investment strategy. The accelerated pace of change serves only to reinforce the importance of focusing on life's priorities: you, your family, and your home; your work, passions, leisure time, and charitable giving; your impact on the world around you. You must manage your money well to achieve what you desire in our uncertain but exciting world.

If beating the market was a central focus of your investing when you first picked up this book, is it still a goal that you care deeply about? Remember that if markets do not care about you, as they surely do not, why should the success of your life's goals depend on their whims?

The markets should simply be one yardstick, albeit an important one, in a larger framework for organizing and managing your financial life—a framework that enables you to remain productively focused on what the money is for.

My sincere hope is that this book has challenged you to think harder, dream bigger, and invest more wisely as you seek answers to these questions. I hope it has also provided you with a simple, intuitive, and implementable investment framework centered on your goals, resources, and aspirations.

Notes

INTRODUCTION

4   *Wealth Allocation Framework*: Ashvin B. Chhabra, "Beyond Markowitz, A Comprehensive Wealth Allocation Framework for Individual Investors," *Journal of Wealth Management* 7, no. 4 (Spring 2005): 8–34. Also available on ssrn.com.

CHAPTER 1: THE INVESTOR'S WORST ENEMY

9   the results are not encouraging: *Dalbar Quantitative Analysis of Investor Behavior Report*, 2014.

9   Standard & Poor's 500 index delivered a very healthy annualized return: For simplicity we will often use the term "annual return" instead of the technically correct term "annualized return." The term refers to the return required each year that would lead to the same total return over the identical time period.

10   between 70 percent and 80 percent identified themselves as above-average drivers: Ola Svenson, "Are We All Less Risky and More Skillful Than Our Fellow Drivers?" *Acta Psychologica* 47, no. 2 (February 1981): 143–48.

10   approximately 88 percent identified themselves as "above-average": Ibid.

11   This is an everyday example of the Dunning-Kruger effect: J. Kruger and D. Dunning, "Unskilled and Unaware of It: How Difficulties in Recognizing One's Own Incompetence Lead to

Inflated Self-Assessments," *Journal of Personality and Social Psychology* 77, no. 6 (December 1999): 1121–34.

12   "The Courage of Misguided Convictions": Brad M. Barber and Terrance Odean, "The Courage of Misguided Convictions," *Financial Analysts Journal* 55, no. 6 (November/December 1999): 41–55.

12   The average return was roughly a *9 percent loss per trade*: The average loss one year later was 3.2 percent plus the transaction cost of the two trades, which at the time of the study was 2.5 percent per trade. Although transaction costs have come down substantially, trading has gotten faster and easier, thus readily enabling a potentially larger number of misguided trades. In fact, when the authors attempted to eliminate trades that may have had more strategic motivations, such as managing taxes and liquidity, the loss percentage actually went up from 3.2 percent to 5.1 percent.

12   Odean and Barber's follow-up paper: Brad M. Barber and Terrance Odean, "Trading Is Hazardous to Your Wealth: The Common Stock Investment Performance of Individual Investors," *Journal of Finance* 55, no. 2 (April 2000): 773–806.

12   have documented this unfortunate finding: Peng Chen, Roger G. Ibbotson, and Kevin X. Zhu, "The ABCs of Hedge Funds: Alphas, Betas, and Costs," *Financial Analysts Journal* 67, no. 1 (January/February 2011): 15–25.

13   out-performance of hedge funds over mutual funds has reversed post-2008: From January 2008 to June 2014, the S&P 500 index delivered a 6.9 percent annualized return with 17.3 percent annualized volatility, the Morningstar US OE Large Blend index returned 5.7 percent with 17.6 percent volatility, the HFRI Fund Weighted Composite index returned 3.0 percent with 7.0 percent volatility, and the HFRX Global Hedge Fund Index returned -1.0 percent with 6.6 percent volatility. Sources: Morningstar, Inc.; Hedge Fund Research, Inc.

13   That's not exactly an attractive value proposition: Charles Ellis, "The Loser's Game," *Financial Analysts Journal* 31, no. 4 (July/August 1975): 19–26. See also Charles Ellis, "The Rise and Fall of Performance Investing," *Financial Analysts Journal* 70, no. 4 (July/August 2014): 14–23.

13   His evidence and conclusions are published in a book that first appeared in 1973, called *A Random Walk Down Wall Street*: Burton Malkiel, *A Random Walk Down Wall Street*, 11th ed. (New York: W. W. Norton & Company, 2015).

14   "precipitating the creation of the world's first index fund": John C. Bogle, "The Professor, the Student, and the Index Fund," http://johncbogle.com/wordpress/wp-content/uploads/2011/09/The-Professor-The-Student-and-the-Index-Fund-9-4-11.pdf.

14   when adjusted for the impact of taxes: Christopher B. Philips, Francis M. Kinniry Jr., Todd Schlanger, and Joshua M. Hirt, "The Case for Index Fund Investing," Vanguard research, April 2014, https://pressroom.vanguard.com/content/nonindexed/Updated_The_Case_for_Index_Fund_Investing_4.9.2014.pdf.

14   would be worth a cool $6,540: Stephen Gandel, "Warren Buffett Is Still a Pretty Good Investor," *Fortune*, May 2, 2014. See also Berkshire Hathaway Shareholder letter 2013, http://www.berkshirehathaway.com/letters/2013ltr.pdf.

15   netted Soros and his investors a billion dollars: Sebastian Mallaby, *More Money Than God: Hedge Funds and the Making of a New Elite* (New York: Penguin Press, 2010), 167.

16   competition pitting active managers against dart throwers: John R. Dorfman, "Pros Gamely Go Up Against Managers," *Wall Street Journal*, October 4, 1988, C1–C2.

16   beating the dart throwers 61 percent of the time: Georgette Jasen, "Journal's Dartboard Retires After 14 Years of Stock Picks," *Wall Street Journal*, April 18, 2002.

17   stocks collectively ended up under-performing the index: Bing Liang, "Price Pressure: Evidence from the 'Dartboard' Column," *Journal of Business* 72, no. 1 (1999): 119–34.

18   "with our colleagues at MarketWatch": Rachel Louise Ensign, "Darts Top Readers in Final Print Contest," *Wall Street Journal*, April 14, 2013.

CHAPTER 2: THE PSYCHOLOGY OF RISK AND REWARD

21   Figure 2.1 "My Wife and My Mother-in-Law, 1889

Anonymous German Postcard": http://en.wikipedia.org/wiki/
My_Wife_and_My_Mother-in-Law.

23   "reptilian brain" wins out over our "rational brain": This is a
glib way of describing what is actually going on. The brain is an
integrated organ, but different parts light up with activity depending on the stimulus and decision to be made. Instinctive, fast
decisions cause certain parts of the brain to be more active while
less urgent decisions requiring more thought cause different parts
of the brain to experience enhanced activity. See, for example:
Daniel Kahneman, *Thinking, Fast and Slow* (New York: Farrar,
Straus and Giroux, 2011).

23   if other managers in the same city were also buying or selling:
Harrison Hong, Jeffrey D. Kubik, and Jeremy C. Stein, "Thy
Neighbor's Portfolio: Word-of-Mouth Effects in the Holdings
and Trades of Money Managers," *Journal of Finance* 60, no. 6
(December 2005): 2801–24.

24   ideas such as asset allocation and diversification: Harry Markowitz, "Portfolio Selection," *Journal of Finance* 7, no. 1 (March
1952): 77–91.

24   hold insurance (safety) and to buy lottery tickets at the same
time: Harry Markowitz, "The Utility of Wealth," *Journal of Political Economy* 60, no. 2 (April 1952): 151–58.

24   the pioneering work of two academic psychologists, Amos Tversky
and Daniel Kahneman: Kahneman, *Thinking, Fast and Slow.*

24   Their work garnered Kahneman the Nobel Prize in Economics in 2002: Tversky did not receive the prize as he died
six years prior to the award. The Nobel Prize is not awarded
posthumously.

25   the *disposition effect*: Hersh Shefrin and Meir Statman, "The Disposition to Sell Winners Too Early and Ride Losers Too Long: Theory
and Evidence," *Journal of Finance* 40, no. 3 (July 1985): 777–90.

25   The lengthy list of behaviorally driven market effects: Nicholas C. Barberis and Richard H. Thaler, "A Survey of Behavioral Finance," in George M. Constantinides, Milton Harris,
and René M. Stulz, eds., *Handbook of the Economics of Finance*,
vol. 1B, *Financial Markets and Asset Pricing* (Amsterdam: Elsevier
North Holland, 2003): 1053–1128

CHAPTER 3: THE VOLATILITY OF MARKETS
OVER A HUMAN LIFETIME

32   the computer, a universal machine: The computer is in effect a universal computing machine and therefore a machine with a programmable chip inside can have a vastly richer set of capabilities than its mechanical analog.

32   happiness and contentment increase with age: "The U-bend of Life," *The Economist*, December 16, 2010, http://www.economist.com/node/17722567.

33   global financial market returns from 1900 to 2000: Elroy Dimson, Paul Marsh, and Mike Staunton, *Triumph of the Optimists: 101 Years of Global Investment Returns* (Princeton, N.J.: Princeton University Press, 2002).

33   urged America to enter the Second World War: Henry R. Luce, "The American Century," *Life*, February 17, 1941, 61–65.

33   even after accounting for inflation: This calculation is for a dollar invested in the stock market from 1900 to 2012 after accounting for inflation. Based on the data available on Professor Robert Shiller's website, http://www.econ.yale.edu/~shiller/data.htm.

33   Russia, India (at that time the crown jewel of the British Empire), and France: Ranking based on gross domestic product (GDP) as a proxy for world markets in 1900. See Dimson, Marsh, and Staunton, *Triumph of the Optimists*, 21, Figure 2-5.

35   a loaf of bread cost 428 billion marks: Robert L. Hetzel, "German Monetary History in the First Half of the Twentieth Century," *Federal Reserve Bank of Richmond Economic Quarterly* 88, no. 1 (Winter 2002): 2.

35   either has ceased to exist or was shut down for some period of time: Philippe Jorion and William M. Goetzmann, "Global Stock Markets in the Twentieth Century," *Journal of Finance* 54, no. 3 (June 1999): 953–80. In an academic paper in which they sought to estimate the long-term return for equity markets around the world, and were thus forced to grapple with this unfortunate reality, the authors found that the lucky countries were able to reopen their stock markets after just a few weeks, albeit with sharply lower prices. But other countries were not so fortunate and stock markets remained closed for months or even years in some cases.

35   "by far the highest uninterrupted real (after inflation) rate of appreciation": Philippe Jorion and William M. Goetzmann, "Global Stock Markets in the Twentieth Century," ibid.

35   Most other countries delivered just a fraction of that: From 1921 to 1996, Jorion and Goetzmann found, the median real return on equities for the thirty-nine countries they studied was just 0.8 percent.

36   Schumpeter's theory of creative destruction: Joseph Schumpeter, *Capitalism, Socialism and Democracy* (New York: Harper & Row, 1975; originally published 1942), 82–85.

36   the only surviving member of the Dow one hundred years later: "The First 120 Years of the Dow Jones," www.quasimodos .com/info/dowhistory.html.

36   biggest initial public offering in US history: Clare Baldwin and Soyoung Kim, "GM IPO Raises $20.1 Billion," Reuters, November 17, 2010.

38   *Irrational Exuberance*: Robert J. Shiller, *Irrational Exuberance*, 2nd ed. (Princeton, N.J.: Princeton University Press, 2006).

40   the work of Professor Shiller: "Long-Term Perspectives on the Current Boom in Home Prices," *Economists' Voice* 3, no. 4 (2006): 1–11.

41   houses in this always fashionable part of the city: One of these houses, built by an upwardly mobile tradesman named Pieter Fransz, still stands today. Piet Eichholtz, "A Long Run House Price Index: The Herengracht Index, 1628–1973," *Real Estate Economics* 25, no. 2 (1997): 175–92.

41   Fig 3.2 is adapted from Robert J. Shiller, "Long-Term Perspectives on the Current Boom in Home Prices," *Economists' Voice* 3, No. 4 (2006): 1-11; and data from Prof. Eichholtz's website at Maastricht University.

41   it would have taken 350 years to double your money: Brent W. Ambrose, Piet Eichholtz, and Thies Lindenthal, "House Prices and Fundamentals: 355 Years of Evidence," *Journal of Money, Credit, and Banking* 45, issue 2–3 (March–April 2013): 477–91.

CHAPTER 4: SPECULATIVE BUBBLES AND MARKET MANIAS

43   this turns out to be a linguistic urban legend: Nicola Di Cosmo,

Luce Foundation Professor in East Asian Studies, Institute for Advanced Study, Princeton, New Jersey, private correspondence.

44   M. C. Escher, *Sky and Water I*, wood print, 1938 (M. C. Escher's *Sky and Water* © 2014, the M. C. Escher Company, the Netherlands. All rights reserved. www.mcescher.com.

45   1841 book, *Extraordinary Popular Delusions and the Madness of Crowds*: Charles Mackay, *Extraordinary Popular Delusions and the Madness of Crowds* (London: Richard Bentley, 1841).

45   "prices fell, and never rose again": This quote was cited in Robert J. Shiller, "From Efficient Markets Theory to Behavioral Finance," *Journal of Economic Perspectives* 17, no. 1 (Winter 2003), 83–104. The original source is Mackay, *Memoirs of Extraordinary Popular Delusions*.

45   desire to enjoy the finer things in life while one could: Jan de Vries and Ad van der Woude, *The First Modern Economy: Success, Failure, and Perseverance of the Dutch Economy* (Cambridge: Cambridge University Press, 1997), 150–51.

46   thanks to the spoils of theft and war: Douglas E. French, *Early Speculative Bubbles and Increases in the Supply of Money*, 2nd ed. (Auburn, Ala.: Ludwig von Mises Institute, 2009), 8.

46   have put forward an alternative thesis: Earl A. Thompson, "The Tulipmania: Fact or Artifact?" *Public Choice* 130, nos. 1–2 (January 2007): 99–114.

46   financial instrument called tulip futures: Christian C. Day, "Is There a Tulip in Your Future?" *Journal des Economistes et des Etudes Humaines* 14, no. 2 (March 2006): 151–70.

47   Those contracts that were not nullified were often unenforceable: Peter M. Garber, "Tulip Mania," *Journal of Political Economy* 97, no. 3 (June 1989): 535–60.

47   economic and social dislocations that upend the existing order: Edward Chancellor, *Devil Take the Hindmost: A History of Financial Speculation* (New York: Plume, June 2000), 92.

47   (and that can be recognized as folly only after the fact): Luboš Pástor and Pietro Veronesi, "Technological Revolutions and Stock Prices," *American Economic Review* 99, no. 4 (2009): 1451–83.

48   less well-known British Railway bubble: Gareth Campbell and John D. Turner, " 'The Greatest Bubble in History': Stock Prices

During the British Railway Mania," SMPRA Paper No. 21820 (2010), http://mpra.ub.uni-muenchen.de/21820/.

48   afflicting US railway stocks from 1873 to 1894: Wikipedia, "Panic of 1893," http://en.wikipedia.org/wiki/Panic_of_1893.

48   most of it on credit: Barry Eichengreen and Kris Mitchener, "The Great Depression as a Credit Boom Gone Wrong," BIS Working Paper No. 137, September 2003.

48   to build 90 million miles of fiber-optic cable: Daniel Gross, "The Fiber-Optic Network Bubble: Back to the Future," *The Milken Institute Review*, March 2002.

50   largest flower auction market in the world: Wikipedia, "Aalsmeer Flower Auction," http://en.wikipedia.org/wiki/Aalsmeer_Flower_Auction.

51   as rational economic theory would suggest: George A. Akerlof and Robert J. Shiller, *Animal Spirits: How Human Psychology Drives the Economy and Why It Matters for Global Capitalism* (Princeton, N.J.: Princeton University Press, 2009), 3.

52   "ignore, exorcise, or condemn those who express doubts": John Kenneth Galbraith, *A Short History of Financial Euphoria* (New York: Whittle Books in association with Viking, 1993), 11.

53   may see their purchasing power and net worth diminish: A more problematic example is the possibility of a broad asset bubble resulting from the easing of credit and related monetary policies by central banks following the 2008 financial crisis. As risky (equity) asset prices rise, investors not participating in the markets may find their net worth decrease relative to those who do participate. This could be further exacerbated if such policies eventually result in higher-than-normal inflation.

CHAPTER 5: HOW DO PEOPLE BECOME (VERY) WEALTHY?

57   The wealth distribution in America stands in sharp contrast: Arthur B. Kennickell, "A Rolling Tide: Changes in the Distribution of Wealth in the U.S., 1989–2001," FEDS Working Paper No. 2003-24, November 2003; Levy Economics Institute Working Paper No. 393. Available at SSRN: http://ssrn.com/abstract=427720.

58   Figure 5.1: The Wealth Spectrum of America: http://www
      .federalreserve.gov/pubs/bulletin/2014/pdf/scf14.pdf.

60   bottom 50 percent hold less than 1 percent of the wealth: *Global
      Wealth Report 2013*, Credit Suisse Research Institute, 2013.

60   inevitable consequence of the capitalistic system: Thomas
      Piketty, *Capital in the Twenty-First Century* (Cambridge, Mass.:
      Harvard University Press, 2014).

61   living on less than a dollar a day: The exact number (and by ex-
      tension percentage) of people who live on less than a dollar a day
      is the subject of much debate and is linked to issues of purchasing
      power parity and how prices around the world are calculated.
      However, the magnitude of the problem of global poverty is
      correctly reflected by this statistic.

63   Cap Gemini World Wealth 2013 report (in conjunction
      with RBC), http://www.capgemini.com/resources/video/
      exploring-the-world-wealth-report-2014.

63   A total of 113 billionaires could not make the list: Kerry A.
      Dolan and Luisa Kroll, "Inside the 2014 Forbes 400: Facts and
      Figures About America's Wealthiest," http://www.forbes.com/
      sites/kerryadolan/2014/09/29/inside-the-2014-forbes-400-
      facts-and-figures-about-americas-wealthiest/.

63   In 1982, its inaugural year: The first Forbes Rich list was pub-
      lished in 1918, but describing the changes would require an-
      other chapter in this book! See http://www.forbes.com/
      video/3819427178001/.

64   "last 25 years in terms of wealth accumulation": Peter Bernstein
      and Annalyn Swan, *All the Money in the World: How the Forbes
      400 Make—and Spend—Their Fortunes* (New York: Vintage,
      2008).

64   roughly equal to the gross domestic product of Russia:
      Luisa Kroll, "Inside the 2013 Forbes 400: Facts and Fig-
      ures On America's Richest," http://www.forbes.com/sites/
      luisakroll/2013/09/16/inside-the-2013-forbes-400-facts-and-
      figures-on-americas-richest/.

64   roughly equal to the gross domestic product of Brazil: Kerry A.
      Dolan and Luisa Kroll, "Inside the 2014 Forbes 400: Facts and Fig-
      ures On America's Wealthiest."

64   business owners, financiers, inheritors, and real estate veterans: The categorization scheme is not unique but it works well. The same categorization is used in Ashvin B. Chhabra, Ravindra Koneru, and Lex Zaharoff, "Modern Portfolio Theory's Third Rail: Achieving Wealth Mobility Through Idiosyncratic Risk," *Journal of Wealth Management* 14, no. 1 (2011): 66–72.

65   most successful hedge fund: Sebastian Mallaby, *More Money Than God: Hedge Funds and the Making of a New Elite* (New York: Penguin Press, 2010).

65   giving away most of his money to scientific research and education: William J. Broad, "Seeker, Doer, Giver, Ponderer: A Billionaire Mathematician's Life of Ferocious Curiosity," *New York Times*, July 7, 2014, D1.

65   "the world's smartest billionaire": Eleanor Lee and Andrea Katz, "The Alternative Rich List," *Financial Times*, September 23, 2006.

67   the least risky strategy: Chhabra et al., "Modern Portfolio Theory's Third Rail: Achieving Wealth Mobility through Idiosyncratic Risk," *Journal of Wealth Management* 14, no. 1 (2011): 66–72.

68   twenty-six people had dropped off the list: Kerry A. Dolan and Luisa Kroll, *Forbes* magazine, "Inside the 2014 Forbes 400: Facts and Figures On America's Wealthiest."

68   next twenty-four consecutive years: Ibid.

68   every year from 1982 to 2003: Lex Zaharoff, "Beating the Odds—Improving the 15 Percent Chance of Staying Wealthy," J.P. Morgan Private Bank Publication, 2006.

CHAPTER 6: HOW MUCH (MONEY) DO I NEED?

73   saved less than $25,000: Ruth Helman, Nevin Adams, Craig Copeland, and Jack VanDerhei, "The 2014 Retirement Confidence Survey: Confidence Rebounds—for Those with Retirement Plans," EBRI Issue Brief, no. 397, March 2014.

74   and live to be ninety: Life expectancy for a newborn in the United States is about 78 years, but one of the interesting facts about life expectancy is that the longer you live, the more your life expectancy improves. Thus at age 60 the average life

expectancy is 22.5, or 82.5 years in total; at 65, the average life expectancy is 18.6 years, or about 83.6 years in total. Adjusted for gender differences, life expectancy at 65 is 82.6 years for a man and 84.6 years for a woman. Based on these statistics, it is reasonable to plan for a life expectancy of 90, but 85 is also defensible.

76   provocative 2006 book called *The Number*: Lee Eisenberg, *The Number: A Completely Different Way to Think About the Rest of Your Life* (New York: Free Press, 2006).

76   "Deep Pockets": Ibid.

78   Maslow's groundbreaking work: A. H. Maslow, "A Theory of Human Motivation," *Psychological Review* 50 (1943), 370–96.

82   the number is $1.25 million: Interestingly, if Mr. Retirement planned for an eighty-five-year life span, the calculation would require the retiree to have about twenty times income—an amount similar to what Eisenberg's friend "Deep Pockets" recommends.

82   Mr. Micawber states in Charles Dickens's classic tale: Charles Dickens, *David Copperfield*, first published in 1849–1850 in the UK by Bradbury & Evans. http://en.wikipedia.org/wiki/David_Copperfield and http://en.wikipedia.org/wiki/Wilkins_Micawber.

83   401(k): For international readers, who may be unfamiliar with the acronym, a 401(k) is a type of a tax-deferred savings plan offered in the United States where the employer will often match an employee's contributions up to a certain amount.

CHAPTER 7: THE WEALTH ALLOCATION FRAMEWORK

88   "is to suggest that there is no such thing": Daniel Kahneman, "The Myth of Risk Attitudes," *Journal of Portfolio Management* 36, no. 1 (Fall 2009): 1.

89   "with the cash he requires to make essential outlays": Robert H. Jeffrey, "A New Paradigm for Risk," *Journal of Portfolio Management* 11, no. 1 (Fall 1984): 33–40.

89   generate cash flow when you need it: In fact, soon after Markowitz published his paper, Tobin recognized the limitation

of simply holding a diversified portfolio, particularly for businesses that had short-term cash-flow obligations that could be well estimated, such as pension payouts. These businesses would be better served by matching their short-term cash obligations using a ladder of Treasury bonds that mature and provide cash flows at the precise time that the obligations need to be paid, thus removing any market risk from defaulting on those payments. This very practical insight led Tobin to a two-portfolio framework consisting of a (risk-less) portfolio of bonds and a (risky) portfolio of market assets. James Tobin, "Liquidity Preference as Behavior Towards Risk," *Review of Economic Studies* 25, no. 1 (1958): 65–86.

The two main questions for the investor, then, are: In what proportion should you divide your wealth among the two portfolios? And what should the composition of the risky portfolio be? This was the origin of the famous two-fund theorem in finance. Tobin eventually won the Nobel Prize in 1981 for his "analysis of financial markets and their relations to expenditure decisions, employment, production and prices."

90   *Risk, Uncertainty and Profit*: Frank H. Knight, *Risk, Uncertainty and Profit* (Boston: Houghton, 1921), available for download at https://mises.org/books/risk_uncertainty_profit_knight.pdf.

90   a variety of subjects, including finance: Mandelbrot coined the word *fractal* in 1975. Benoit B. Mandelbrot, *The Fractal Geometry of Nature* (San Francisco: W. H. Freeman, 1977).

90   "mildly random but *wildly* random": Benoit B. Mandelbrot, "New Methods in Statistical Economics," *Journal of Political Economy* 71, no. 5 (October 1963): 421–40. See also Benoit Mandelbrot and Richard L. Hudson, *The (Mis)behavior of Markets: A Fractal View of Risk, Ruin, and Reward* (New York: Basic Books, 2004).

91   author of *The Black Swan*: Nassim Nicholas Taleb, *The Black Swan: The Impact of the Highly Improbable* (New York: Random House, 2007).

91   reinterpreted by self-serving experts as such: This refers to the power of creating a story to make sense of our past, present, and

future. This characteristic seems to be a universal need in all humans (not just experts), embedded deep in our nature. Culture, religion, and history are all different aspects of this phenomenon. See George A. Akerlof and Robert J. Shiller, *Animal Spirits: How Human Psychology Drives the Economy, and Why It Matters for Global Capitalism* (Princeton, N.J.: Princeton University Press, 2009), and David Tuckett, *Minding the Markets: An Emotional Finance View of Financial Instability* (Basingstoke: Palgrave Macmillan, 2011).

92   seminal paper on Prospect Theory: Daniel Kahneman and Amos Tversky, *Prospect Theory: An Analysis of Decision Making under Risk, Econometrica* 47, no. 2 (March 1979): 263–92.

92   cannot be diversified away through portfolio optimization: Market risk, or beta, cannot be diversified away in a long-only portfolio, but a long-short portfolio can be constructed with no systematic exposure to the market. This concept is explored more deeply in Chapter 8.

CHAPTER 8: DIGGING DEEPER

105   at an inflection point: See, for example, Andy Grove, *Only the Paranoid Survive: How to Identify and Exploit the Crisis Points That Challenge Every Business* (New York: Doubleday, 1999).

106   employer stock and stock options is a fundamentally risky propostion: Stock options have leverage built into their structure and therefore serve only to magnify the risk-reward trade-offs of owning company stock. These are valuable and also subject to misuse: see Ashvin B. Chhabra, "Executive Stock Options: Moral Hazard or Just Compensation?" *Journal of Wealth Management* 11, no. 1 (Summer 2008): 20–35.

106   assets such as employer stock and stock options, generally speaking, belong in the aspirational bucket: Bear in mind that these assets—if you own them—are often highly correlated to your personal income stream, or human capital, thus amplifying their risk.

109   physical gold should yield a return consistent with inflation: Technical considerations such as holding costs and taxation on gold bars may lower this rate of return to below inflation.

109 Thus gold held for the diversification benefit belongs in the market bucket: Holding gold stocks is often a leveraged play on the price of gold. Investors must understand that such exposure provides an asymmetric payoff relative to the price of production for each specific company as well as the usual price considerations of when you bought the stock.

109 nontraditional investments such as hedge funds: The grouping of hedge funds under alternative investments is by convention, but it does not adequately capture the true nature of that investment. A hedge fund is a partnership with a specific investment strategy. There are two sources of risk and return—the strategy itself and the partnership.

CHAPTER 9: SEVEN STEPS TO IMPLEMENTATION

122 *zero discount method* to quantify the total amount needed *today*: A more advanced version of this methodology involves not only differentiating among essential, important, and aspirational goals, but also differentiating the essential, important, and aspirational *expenditures within each goal.*

124 The adjustment factor: In this case the adjustment factor would be 80 percent if one assumed that 20 percent of retirement income would come from a pension or special security. Similarly one would make a further reduction if one assumed investment gains over and above inflation.

125 adaptibility and flexibility are key: In addition to updating a table summarizing your goals and related cash flows, it is essential on an annual basis to ensure that you have your legal documents in order and that you are taking full advantage of year-end tax breaks afforded by vehicles such as 401(k) contributions and employer matches, that you have made insurance payments for health, home, auto, and life insurance, and that your wills, living trust, and powers of attorney for health decisions are up to date.

127 sixty thousand respondents from 123 countries: Louis Tay and Ed Diener, "Needs and Subjective Well-Being Around the World," *Journal of Personality and Social Psychology* 101, no. 2 (2011): 354–65.

127 "we need them all": Hans Villarica, "Maslow 2.0: A New and Improved Recipe for Happiness," The Atlantic.com, August 17, 2011, http://www.theatlantic.com/health/archive/2011/08/maslow-20-a-new-and-improved-recipe-for-happiness/243486/.

CHAPTER 10: OWNING THE WORLD

140 the rest is history: Interview with Harry Markowitz conducted on October 8, 2004, at the Rady School of Management, University of California, San Diego, by Steve Buser, on behalf of the American Finance Association: www.afajof.org.
MARKOWITZ: So I went to my advisor, Professor Jacob Marschak. He was busy when I got there, so I waited in his anteroom. There was another fellow in the anteroom who turned out to be a broker waiting for Marschak. We chatted while we were there, and he suggested that I should maybe do a dissertation on the stock market. So I went in.
BUSER: A stockbroker gave you the idea? . . . A tip that paid off.
MARKOWITZ: Yeah. Some biographer of mine said this was the best advice a stockbroker has ever given. And I agree.

141 he chose standard deviation: Standard deviation is the square root of a quantity called variance. Variance is thus the square of standard deviation. We will use these terms interchangeably to denote risk in the Markowitz framework.

141 as his measure of choice: As Peter Bernstein points out in his book *Against the Gods: The Remarkable Story of Risk* (New York: John Wiley & Sons, 1996), Markowitz refers to risk as "variance of return," the "undesirable thing" that investors seek to minimize.

143 *The Rise and Decline of the Medici Bank*: Raymond de Roover, *The Rise and Decline of the Medici Bank: 1397–1494* (Cambridge, Mass.: Harvard University Press, 1963).

143 *Merchant of Venice*: William Shakespeare, *The Merchant of Venice* (~1596).

145 market-weighted world equity index: There is a debate to be had about what index would be the best choice, but a market-weighted one, that is, weighted by a company's market capitalization, is a

reasonably good default option. Indeed, efficient market purists will argue that it is the only option.

146 Sharpe ratio: The Sharpe ratio is defined as the excess return of the portfolio over the risk-free rate divided by the volatility of the portfolio. This risk-adjusted measure was first proposed by Nobel laureate William Sharpe and is widely used to evaluate the portfolio returns of managers taking on different levels of market risk.

146 "variation in total plan return": Gary P. Brinson, L. Randolph Hood, and Gilbert L. Beebower, "Determinants of Portfolio Performance," *Financial Analysts Journal* 42, no. 4 (July/August 1986): 39–44.

147 the alpha generated by your portfolio will be small: Pension funds by their nature do not take big bets and often (explicitly or implicitly) discourage their managers from doing so. Thus it is no surprise that when looking at pension fund portfolios, the monthly returns were closely correlated to the returns of the underlying asset allocations.

147 strategic asset allocation will largely determine your total return: Here it is useful to use a measure of a portfolio's sensitivity to the equity market, known as beta. A 100 percent equity diversified portfolio has on average a beta of 1, a diversified portfolio split 60:40 between equities and bonds has a beta of roughly 0.6, and a portfolio split 40:60 between equities and bonds has a 0.4 beta. For a standard stock and bond portfolio, you simply compute the beta of the portfolio and multiply it by how the market did over time. That should give you a rough estimate of your return and also will provide a good idea of the variation (volatility) of the returns with regard to the market. A 1-beta portfolio should track the equity market while a 0.5-beta portfolio should have roughly half the upside and downside. The difference between the actual return and the beta-estimated return is the total alpha—the net return from all active management bets that you hope is positive. For simplicity, I have glossed over the effects of correlation in these estimates of beta, and the relationships described above are statistical.

148 they either consciously or subconsciously begin to hug their underlying benchmarks: For a definition of active risk taking relative to a benchmark or "active share," see Martijn Cremers and

Antti Petajisto, "How Active Is Your Fund Manager? A New Measure That Predicts Performance," March 31, 2009, http://ssrn.com/abstract=891719.

149   managed to both endure and establish a decade-and-a-half track record of outperformance: Christopher B. Philips, Francis M. Kinniry Jr., Todd Schlanger, and Joshua M. Hirt, "The Case for Index Fund Investing," Vanguard research, April 2014, https://pressroom.vanguard.com/content/nonindexed/Updated_The_Case_for_Index_Fund_Investing_4.9.2014.pdf.

149   surest path to sustainable returns: One important area where the Wealth Allocation Framework differs from Brinson's conclusions is that, from the lens of the framework, determining the correct asset allocation is not the most important role for the committee. Instead, it should be to develop an investment strategy that is in line with the goals of the institution.

150   *The Wisdom of Crowds*: James Surowiecki, *The Wisdom of Crowds* (New York: Anchor Books, 2005).

151   Figure 10.3: Proxy for Equities is S&P 500 Index; for Fixed Income, it is the Barclays US Aggregate Bond Index; for Cash, it is the Ibbotson's 30-Day Treasury Bill Index; for Hedge Funds, it is the HFRI Fund Weighted Composite Index; for Commodities, it is the Goldman Sachs Commodity Index.

CHAPTER 11: DO NOT TRY THIS AT HOME

160   beginning of 1965 through the end of 2013: *Berkshire Hathaway Inc. 2013 Annual Report*, p. 2.

160   about on par with the 26.2 percent loss for the S&P index that year: Results for Fiscal Year 2009, that is, July 1, 2008, to June 30, 2009.

161   got a good reception from fixed income investors: Gillian Wee, "Harvard, Yale Endowments Decline 30 percent on Private-Equity Losses," *Bloomberg News*, September 11, 2009. "Harvard was forced to fire workers, sold $2.5 billion in bonds, and delayed construction projects after the bankruptcy of Lehman Brothers Holdings Inc. in September 2008 crippled financial markets and left the 373-year-old university short of cash."

161   actually concentrated in the market portfolio: This viewpoint

is consistent with David Swensen's own interpretation of the strategy as elaborated in his book *Pioneering Portfolio Management: An Unconventional Approach to Institutional Investment* (New York: Free Press, 2000).

161 "(but still require exposure to the equity market)": Berkshire Hathaway Annual Letter 1993. "Another situation requiring wide diversification occurs when an investor who does not understand the economics of specific businesses nevertheless believes that it is in his interest to be a long-term owner of American industry. That investor should both own a large number of equities and space out his purchases. By periodically investing in an index fund, for example, the know-nothing investor can actually outperform most investment professionals. Paradoxically, when 'dumb' money acknowledges its limitations, it ceases to be dumb."

162 far superior to the mean performance of a broad range of university endowments: Yale Endowment Report 2009.

163 "well-thought-out investing strategy": Swensen, *Pioneering Portfolio Management*, 3–7. The reader is well advised to read the entire book.

166 "developed by Nobel laureates James Tobin and Harry Markowitz": 2013 Yale Endowment Report, http://investments.yale.edu/images/documents/Yale_Endowment_13.pdf.

166 Figure 11.3: This is a rough estimate by the author based on publicly available data. The conclusions outlined in the chapter do not depend on the exact numbers.

167 *significant wealth over the long haul*: As one goes carefully through each strategy or pie slice, one sees that they are carefully structured investing strategies using traditional assets. There are changes in parts of the strategy to reduce beta and increase alpha, which in turn come with leverage and idiosyncratic risk or illiquidity. In recognition of that aspect of risk management, most of these tweaks are kept in perspective. For example, a long-short manager is often benchmarked against an equity index, so he or she may leverage up to 200 percent but not much more. The funds' beta exposures may go to 0.5 but not much less. Venture capital funds provide the potential for singular, spectacular investments but the size of any single investment is constrained by the need to diversify at the early stage across many

investments. The managers thus deliver better risk-return than most indices or underlying benchmarks, but the approximate profile of each sleeve is still the market bucket.

167   over a period of five to fifteen years: The returns of venture capital on a whole have disappointed. See for example: Harold S. Bradley, Diane Mulcahy, and Bill Weeks, "'We Have Met the Enemy . . . and He Is Us': Lessons from Twenty Years of the Kauffman Foundation's Investments in Venture Capital Funds and the Triumph of Hope over Experience," Kauffman Foundation, May 2012.

168   Figure 11.4 is based on information contained in Yale University Annual Endowment Reports.

169   access to the top investment managers in the world: In fact, an investment from the Yale endowment adds prestige to any investment organization or manager. Yale has used this clout to negotiate favorable terms for its investments. The endowment also makes a conscious effort to identify talented managers at an early stage in their careers and adopt a carrot-and-stick approach, helping the manager set up a top-quality, sustainable organization and providing seed capital but also negotiating favorable terms and limiting the amount of money the manager could accept from other investors. Asset size is a known enemy of excess returns, and Yale has gone to great lengths to earn the latter.

172   "next generation," actively managed market portfolios: For most top-tier educational institutions, the donor base as well as land and university buildings provide further diversification. As a well-known Ivy League professor once reminded me, these universities could easily double their tuition without fearing that they would not be able to fill every available seat.

172   "stress beta" of the portfolio turned out to be about 1: Martin L. Leibowitz, Anthony Bova, and P. Brett Hammond, *The Endowment Model of Investing: Return, Risk, and Diversification* (Hoboken, N.J.: John Wiley & Sons, 2010).

174   "buffers for the investment pool": Karen W. Arenson, "Q&A; A Modest Proposal," *New York Times*, August 2, 1998. See also: Henry Hansmann, "Why Do Universities Have Endowments?," *Journal of Legal Studies* 19, no. 1 (January 1990): 3–42.

174   *Security Analysis*: Benjamin Graham and David Dodd, *Security Analysis* (New York: McGraw-Hill, 1934).

175 "this particular intellectual village": Warren E. Buffett, "The Superinvestors of Graham-and-Doddsville," *Hermes, the Columbia Business School Magazine*, 1984, 4–15.

176 to ketchup maker Heinz: *Berkshire Hathaway Inc. 2013 Annual Report*, 4.

176 Buffett himself describes as a "core operation": Ibid., 7.

176 "insurers get to invest this float for their benefit": *Berkshire Hathaway Inc. 2013 Annual Report*, 7.

178 to more than $48 billion as of early 2014: Matt Philips, "A Brief History of Warren Buffett's Berkshire Hathaway, as Told Through Its Giant Cash Pile," *Quartz*, May 5, 2014.

178 $26.7 billion purchase of Burlington Northern: "Buffett Buying Burlington Northern Railroad," Associated Press, November 3, 2009, http://www.nbcnews.com/id/33599744/ns/business-us_business/t/buffett-buying-burlington-northern-railroad/#.U63fWI1dWFM.

178 at least $20 billion in cash in reserve: "Berkshire Opposes Dividend Proposal; Buffett, Gates Get Pay Rises," Reuters, March 16, 2014, http://www.reuters.com/article/2014/03/16/us-berkshire-dividend-idUSBREA2F0N220140316.

178 book value increased by about 84 percent: Jeff Sommer, "The Oracle of Omaha, Lately Looking a Bit Ordinary," *New York Times*, April 5, 2014. http://www.nytimes.com/2014/04/06/business/the-oracle-of-omaha-lately-looking-a-bit-ordinary.html.

178 has not done since 1967 and Buffett opposes: "Berkshire Opposes Dividend Proposal; Buffett, Gates Get Pay Rises," Reuters, March 16, 2014, http://www.reuters.com/article/2014/03/16/us-berkshire-dividend-idUSBREA2F0N220140316.

178 "The stock market is a voting machine rather than a weighing machine": Graham and Dodd, *Security Analysis*, 6th ed. (New York: McGraw Hill, 2009): 497. First published in 1934.

179 roughly twice the return of S&P 500: See, for example, Berkshire Hathaway's shareholder letter for 2013 that provides a comparison of the compounded return of the firm's book value (19.7 percent) with that of the S&P 500, including dividends (9.8 percent). Available at http://www.berkshirehathaway.com/letters/2013ltr.pdf.

179 well-chosen but illiquid equity–heavy portfolio with no safety

net: refers to the fact that the sources of risk in the portfolio are directly or closely related to the valuation of the equity risk premium.

179   in a precarious position: Indeed many universities resorted to lay-offs during the crisis, abandoning lower-paid and vulnerable staff at the most critical time. Others postponed critical projects that were central to their mission. The arms race had its victims and many of them would have preferred not to participate.

180   "Do no try this at home": Marc Gunther, "Yale's $8 Billion Man. Yale's David Swensen has made better returns than any portfolio manager at any University. He has a word of advice: don't try this at home," *Yale Alumni Magazine*, July/August 2005.

Index

Pages numbers followed by *f* and n indicate figures and notes.

active management, of investments
efficient market debate and, 2–3, 13–18
manager alpha and market beta and, 65, 110–12, 141–42, 145–49, 204n
as zero-sum game, 12, 147
see also Endowment model of investing; professional advisors
Against the Gods: The Remarkable Story of Risk (Bernstein), 203n
aggressive risk allocation, 131, 131*f*
agrarian age, dominant economies in, 31
agricultural revolution, 185
All the Money in the World (Bernstein and Swan), 63–64, 68
alpha
active management and, 110–12, 147–49, 204n
long-short funds and, 112–14
alternative investments
allocated to risk buckets, 97–98, 109–14
Endowment model of investing and, 159, 163–64
ambiguity, risk/reward and resolving of, 21–23, 21*f*

Amsterdam
real estate values in, 37–41, 40*f*, 107
tulip bulb bubble and, 46, 50
anchoring, in behavioral finance, 25
angel investments, allocated to risk bucket, 98
"animal spirits," Keynes and, 47, 51
annuities, allocated to risk buckets, 97
aspirational goals
in objective-driven investing, 122, 123*f*, 126*f*, 127
as principal objective of investing, 91–92
for retirement, 80
aspirational risk bucket and portfolio
asset allocation and, 94, 95, 97–98, 132, 134
caution about, 140
difficult-to-classify asset allocation, 103–5, 103*f*, 106, 108, 109, 113–16
performance measurement and, 116–18
purpose of, 93, 93*f*, 94
reviewing and rebalancing of, 136–37, 137*f*
stress tests and, 135

aspirational risk bucket and portfolio
 (*continued*)
   Wealth Allocation snapshot and,
     128

bankruptcy, in US, 61–62
Barber, Brad, 11–12, 111
Barclays Aggregate Bond Index, 10, 14
"beating the market"
   achieving goals versus, 3, 18, 116,
     183, 186
   Berkshire Hathaway and, 14–15
   efficient frontier and, 88
   Malkiel and, 13
   market portfolio construction
     and, 146, 154, 163
   Wall Street Journal dart throwers
     and, 16–18
Beebower, Gilbert, 146–47
behavioral finance, 2, 3, 192n
biases as risk/reward trade-offs,
     24–26
   complex attitudes toward risk
     and, 88–89
   determining ability to bear loses,
     128, 130–31, 131*f*
   speculative bubbles and, 51–53, 52*f*
benchmarks
   alpha and beta and, 110–11,
     145–50
   fund performance and, 12
   performance measurement and,
     116–17
Berkshire Hathaway. *See* value
   investing
Bernstein, Peter, 63–64, 68, 203n
beta
   active management and, 110–12,
     141–42, 147–49, 204n
   long-short investing, 112–14,
     201n
   BH Reinsurance, 177
*Black Swan: The Impact of the
   Highly Improbable, The* (Taleb),
     90–91
Bogle, Jack, 14

Bonderman, David, 65
bond funds
   annual returns and, 10
   diversification and, 141–42,
     144–45, 149, 152
   Endowment model and, 160–64,
     171–72
   investment allocations and, 14,
     87, 97, 117
Boston College, Center for Retire-
     ment Research at, 73
Brinson, Gary, 146–47, 205n
British Railway bubble, 47–48
bubbles, in market. *See* speculative
   bubbles
bubonic plague, tulip bulb bubble
   and, 45–46
Buffett, Warren, 14–15, 65
   diversification and, 161, 205–6n
   see also value investing
bull markets, questionable invest-
     ment decisions and, 62
Burlington Northern Railroad, 178
business cycles, average returns
     across, 151–52, 151*f*
businesses
   owners, on Forbes 400 list, 64–65
   private, allocated to aspirational
     risk bucket, 98, 103–5, 103*f*

Cap Gemini World Wealth 2013
   report, 63
capital calls, in private equity, 114,
     160–61
capitalism, wealth distribution and,
     60
cash
   allocated to risk buckets, 97, 116
   in Berkshire Hathaway portfolio,
     178, 179
   converting goals into cash flow, 122,
     124, 125, 126*f*, 127, 202n
   event risk and availability of,
     89–90
   in investment portfolio, generally,
     14, 140

positive cash flow as important
retirement goal, 83–84
Center for Retirement Research, at
Boston College, 73
Chen, Peng, 12
China, changing economic conditions in, 31, 34
cognitive dissonance, in behavioral
finance, 25
college. *See* education
"Comfortable" lifestyle, in retirement, 76
"Comfortable Plus" lifestyle, in
retirement, 76
commodities, speculative bubbles
and, 51
computer, as universal machine, 32,
193n
concentration, in investing, 3,
14–15
Forbes 400 list and, 67, 69–70
home ownership and, 107
conflicts of interest, minimized in
Yale endowment, 163
conservative risk allocation, 131,
131*f*
constant purchasing power, retirement planning and, 81–84
contrarian investing, alpha and,
147–48
control, behavioral finance and illusion of, 25, 98, 104–5
correlation, as dimension of risk, 88
cost of living
market risk bucket and, 92, 201n
retirement savings and, 82
see also living standards
"Courage of Misguided Convictions, The" (Barber and
Odean), 11–12, 190n
creative destruction, economic
power changes and, 36
currency trading, in Wealth Allocation Framework, 115
customized investment vehicles, in
Yale endowment, 163

David Copperfield (Dickens), 82
dead funds, 148–49
debt
allocated to risk buckets, 96, 97, 108
impact on retirement goals,
82–84
objective-driven investing, 144
real estate and leveraging of, 37, 170
Wealth Allocation snapshot and,
127
de Roover, Raymond, 143
Dickens, Charles, 82
Di Cosmo, Nicola, 43
"difficult to quantify risks test," of
Wealth Allocation Framework,
136
digital revolution, economic
changes and, 31–32, 185
Dimson, Elroy, 33–34
disposition effect, in behavioral
finance, 25
diversification
asset allocation and, 134
Buffett and, 161, 205–6n
Forbes 400 list and, 69–70
Markowitz's efficient frontier and,
140–44, 143*f*
in modern portfolio theory, 24, 88
as traditional investing advice, 3,
13–14, 16
Dodd, David, 174
dollar, change in value of, 33, 193n
Dow Jones Industrial Average, 35, 36
Dunning, David, 11
Dunning-Kruger effect, in trading, 11
du Pont, John E., 68
Dutch tulip bulb bubble, 45–47, 50

education
debt for, allocated to risk buckets,
97
human capital and, 115–16, 132
saving for college and, 124, 152
efficient frontier, 88–89, 203n
active management debate and,
2–3, 13–18

efficient frontier *(continued)*
  asset allocation and, 144–49,
    144*f*
  basics of, 140–44, 143*f*
  wealth creation and, 89–90
Eichholtz, Piet, 40–41
Eisenberg, Lee, 76–77
Ellis, Charles, 13
Employee Benefit Research Insti-
    tute, 73
endowment bias, in behavioral
    finance, 25
Endowment model of investing, 112
  alternative investments and, 159,
    163–64
  Harvard and Yale policy portfo-
    lios, 165*f*
  performance of (2000–2009),
    159, 162, 162*f*
  risk allocation, of typical Ivy
    League university, 173*f*
  versus traditional portfolio, 166*f*,
    168*f*, 170*f*
  2008 financial crisis and, 160–61,
    164–74, 170*f*, 205n
  Wealth Allocation Framework
    and risk allocation, 161, 164–74,
    173*f*, 179–80, 207n
England, changing economic condi-
    tions in, 31, 33–34
equity fund investments, annual
    returns and, 9–10
equity risk premium, Endowment
    model and, 163, 166–67,
    208n
Escher, M. C., 44, 44*f*
essential goals
  in objective-driven investing,
    122, 123*f*, 125, 126*f*, 127
  for retirement, 79, 80
event risk, cash availability and,
    89–90
*Extraordinary Popular Delusions and
    the Madness of Crowds* (Mackay),
    45

*Federal Reserve Survey of Consumer
  Finances, The*, 57

fees
  lost returns and, 9–10
  of managed funds, 12–13, 98,
    113, 148–49
fiber-optic cable bubble, 48
Fidelity Investments, 65
Financial Analysts Journal, 146–47
financial crisis of 2008
  company stocks and, 106
  effects on Endowment model of
    investing, 160–61, 164–74, 170*f*,
    205n
  Forbes 400 list and, 64
  hedge funds and, 13
  home prices and, 107
  United States and, 35, 73, 196n
financial safety, balancing with
    wealth creation, 4–5
529 plans, tax-aware investing and, 152
fixed income securities, allocated to
    risk buckets, 97, 98
"float," value to Berkshire Hathaway
    portfolio, 176
Forbes 400 list, 60, 75
  average net worth of individuals
    on, 63–64
  investment strategies and, 66–68
  sources of wealth of individuals
    on, 64–66
  volatility of list, 67–70
401(k) savings plans, 83, 152, 199n
fractal geometry, Mandelbrot and, 90
framing, in behavioral finance, 25
France, changing economic condi-
    tions in, 33–35
futures contracts, tulip bulb bubble
    and, 46–47

Gates, Bill, 65
GEICO, 177
General Electric, 36, 178
General Motors, 36
General Re, 177
Germany, changing economic con-
    ditions in, 34–35
goals
  achieving, versus beating the
    market, 3, 18, 116, 183, 186

converting cash flow into, 122, 124–25, 126*f*, 127
    outlining of, 122, 123*f*
Goetzmann, William M., 193n, 194n
gold, allocated to risk buckets, 108–9, 201n, 202n
Goldman Sachs, 178
Graham, Benjamin, 174, 178–79
greater fool syndrome, speculative bubbles and, 53
Gross, Bill, 65
"groupthink," versus "wisdom of crowds," 150

Hansmann, Henry, 172, 174
Harvard University
    endowment growth (2000–2009), 159
    manager selection and, 168–69, 207n
    policy portfolio of, 164, 165*f*
    2008 financial crisis and, 160–61, 205n
hedge funds
    allocated to risk buckets, 97, 109–14, 202n
    performance and, 12–13, 190n
herd mentality, market bubbles and, 23–24, 52
"Herengracht Index," 40–41, 40*f*
Hermes (magazine), Buffett article in, 174–75
hierarchy of needs, of Maslow, 78–79, 78*f*, 127
high-net-worth individuals, world-wide, 63
home. *See* residences
Hood, L. Randolph, 146–47
housing bubble, in US, 49–50
human capital (earnings potential)
    allocated to risk buckets, 97, 103*f*, 115–16, 164
    cash flow and, 125
    importance of, 101
    monetizing of, 65, 66–67, 184
    risk tolerance and, 132
humanistic psychology, 78
Hunt, Ray Lee, 68

Ibbotson, Roger, 12
idiosyncratic risk
    aspirational risk and, 93, 117
    diversification away from, 109, 142, 145
    Endowment model and 2008 financial crisis, 167, 206n
illiquidity premium
    market portfolio construction and, 149–50
    Yale endowment and, 163, 169
illusion of control, in behavioral finance, 25, 98, 104–5
illusion of superiority
    speculative bubbles and, 53
    in trading, 11
important goals
    in objective-driven investing, 122, 123*f*, 125, 126*f*, 127
    for retirement, 79–80
indexing of investments and index funds, 113–14, 154
    alpha and beta and, 110–11
    benefits of, 205–6n
    efficient market hypothesis and, 2–3, 13–14, 16–17
    "Herengracht Index" and, 40–41, 40*f*
    market portfolio and, 145, 149, 203n
India, changing economic conditions in, 31, 33–34
Industrial Revolution, economic changes and, 31, 60, 185
inflation
    gold and, 108–9, 201n
    objective-driven investing, 146
    retirement planning and, 5, 74, 81–84
    return on investments and, 9, 10, 33, 35, 40, 97, 111
    safety and, 117
information
    confusion from abundance of, 2
    information advantages and risk, 89–90
    perspective and interpretation of, 22

information age, and "mass customization" concept, 185
inheritance, Forbes 400 list and, 64, 66
innovation, speculative bubbles and, 46–47
instinct versus reason, in trading, 23, 192n
insurance
    allocated to personal risk bucket, 97
    value to Berkshire Hathaway portfolio, 176
Internet bubble, 35, 48, 49*f*
investment strategies, generally
    principal objectives of, 91–92
    selling assets with little return potential, 96
    selling concentrated stock positions, 106
    see also specific strategies
investors, 9–27
    ambiguity and, 21–23, 21*f*
    concentration and, 3, 14–16
    efficient market versus active management and, 13–18
    herd mentality and, 23–24, 52
    inaccurate perceptions of results, 10–11
    market reversion beliefs and, 26–27
    poor results of institutional and managed investing, 12–13, 190n
    poor trading decisions in self-directed investing, 11–12, 111
    underperformance and, 9–10
    see also behavioral finance
Irrational Exuberance (Shiller), 38

Japan, changing economic conditions in, 34
Jeffrey, Robert, 89
jelly bean experiment, 150
Johnson, Abigail, 65
Johnson, Edward III, 65
Jorion, Philippe, 193n, 194n

Journal of Finance, 24
Journal of Political Economy, 24

Kahneman, Daniel, 24–25, 88–89, 192n
Keynes, John Maynard, 51, 77
"Kind of Rich" lifestyle, in retirement, 76
Knight, Frank, 90, 92, 94
Kruger, Justin, 11

legal documents, importance of keeping in order, 202n
leverage
    embedded, and private businesses, 104
    Endowment model and 2008 financial crisis, 167, 206n
    Forbes 400 list and, 67, 69–70
    real estate and, 37, 107
liability allocation, in Wealth Allocation Framework, 96–97
life expectancy, 132, 198n
lifestyle. *See* living standards
liquid investments, allocated to personal risk bucket, 95
living standards
    Eisenberg's list of retirement lifestyles, 76–77
    investment goals and, 4–5
    market portfolio construction and, 149
    objective-driven investing, 132
    personal risk bucket and, 92
    retirement planning and, 73
loans. *See* debt
long-short investing, 110–14
    Endowment model and, 167, 206n
    market alpha and, 112–14
"Loser's Game, The" (Ellis), 13
loss aversion, in behavioral finance, 25
losses, determining financial and psychological ability to bear, 128, 130–31, 131*f*
"loss of employment test," of Wealth Allocation Framework, 135
Luce, Henry, 33

Mackay, Charles, 45
Malkiel, Burton, 13–14
"manager selection," Endowment
    model and, 168, 168*f*, 170, 207n
Mandelbrot, Benoit, 90–91, 92, 94
manias. *See* speculative bubbles
"market meltdown test," of Wealth
    Allocation Framework, 135
market-neutral funds, 113
market risk bucket and portfolio,
    139–55
    active and passive management
      decisions, 145–49
    asset allocation and, 95, 97–98, 134
    business cycles and time and,
      151–52, 151*f*
    difficult-to-classify asset allo-
      cation, 103*f*, 106, 108, 109,
      114–15, 116
    efficient market theory and,
      140–45, 143*f*, 203n
    expensive and illiquid asset classes
      and, 149–50
    performance measurement and,
      116–18
    purpose of, 92, 93*f*, 94
    reviewing and rebalancing of,
      136–37, 137*f*, 145, 152–54, 153*f*
    simple versus complex models,
      144*f*
    standard of living and, 149
    volatility and, 150–51
    Wealth Allocation snapshot and,
      128
markets
    bubble drivers and examples,
      43–50
    economic dynamics of bubbles,
      50–54
    volatility and changing fortunes
      of countries and businesses,
      31–37
    volatility of all, 35, 193n
    volatility of real estate values as
      example, 37–41
market-weighted equity index, 145,
    203n

Markowitz, Harry, 109, 166
    modern portfolio theory and, 24,
      87–88, 90, 140–45, 143*f*, 203n
    Wealth Allocation Framework
      and, 92, 94
Marsh, Paul, 33–34
Maslow, Abraham, and hierarchy of
    needs, 78–79, 78*f*, 127
"mass customization" concept,
    185–86
mean reversion
    rates of return and, 26–27
    real estate values and, 41
    Yale endowment portfolio and, 166
mean-variance framework, of Mar-
    kowitz, 88, 142, 166
Merchant of Venice (Shakespeare),
    143–44
Meyer, Jack, 159
moderate risk allocation, 131, 131*f*
modern portfolio theory
    basics of, 4, 13–18, 24, 101
    complex attitudes toward risk
      and, 88–89
    event risk and cash flow and, 89–90
    extreme adverse market moves
      and, 90–91
    volatility and risk and, 87–88
    Wealth Allocation Framework
      and, 92, 94, 117
    see also efficient frontier
moral hazard, speculative bubbles
    and, 52
mortgage debt, allocated to personal
    risk bucket, 97, 108
municipal bonds, tax-aware invest-
    ing and, 152
mutual funds, underperformance
    and, 12–13, 190n
"Myth of Risk Attitudes, The"
    (Kahneman), 88–89

NASDAQ stock market, collapse of,
    48, 49*f*
"Neighbor's Portfolio, Thy" study, 23
neuroeconomics. *See* behavioral
    finance

Newton, Isaac, 47
"Number, the." *See* retirement
    planning

objective-driven investing, 4, 128, 187
    advantages of, 121–22
Odean, Terry, 11–12, 111
overconfidence, in behavioral fi-
    nance, 25, 53, 98

personal risk bucket. *See* safety risk
    bucket and portfolio
Piketty, Thomas, 60
PIMCO, 65
Pioneering Portfolio Management
    (Swenson), 163
policy portfolio, 147
    Yale and Harvard endowments
    and, 164, 165*f*
"Portfolio Selection" (Markowitz), 24
positive cash flow, as important
    retirement goal, 83–84
principle-protected notes, allocated
    to risk bucket, 97
private equity
    allocated to risk bucket, 114–15
    Endowment model and 2008 fi-
    nancial crisis, 160–61, 167, 169,
    170*f*, 171, 205n
professional advisors
    versus dart throwers, 16–18
    focus of, 2–3
    modern portfolio theory and
    efficient frontier, 87–88
    underperformance and costs and,
    12–13, 190n
    see also active management, of
    investments
Prospect Theory, of Kahnemann
    and Tversky, 88–89, 92
psychology of investing. See behav-
    ioral finance; risk and reward,
    psychology of

railroad bubble, 47–48
Random Walk Down Wall Street, A
    (Malkiel), 13–14

"rational brain," reason and instinct
    and, 23, 26, 192n
real estate investments
    allocated to risk buckets, 97, 98,
    103*f*, 107–8
    Endowment model of investing
    and, 169, 171
    Forbes 400 list and, 64, 66
    returns over time, 37–41, 39*f*
real estate investment trusts
    (REITs), 108
reason versus instinct, in trading, 23,
    26, 192n
rebalancing, of market portfolio
    objective-driven investing,
    136–37, 137*f*, 145, 152, 153*f*, 154
    weakness of market timing and, 26
    Wealth Allocation Framework
    and, 87, 133
recessions, questionable investment
    decisions and, 62
regret aversion, in behavioral fi-
    nance, 25–26
rental properties, allocated to risk
    buckets, 108
representativeness bias, in behavioral
    finance, 25
"reptilian brain," reason and instinct
    and, 23, 26, 192n
residences
    home ownership and risk buckets,
    97, 107
    renting of, 107
retirement planning, 73–84
    calculating needed savings,
    73–74, 77
    essential, important, and aspira-
    tional goals and, 79–80
    prioritizing of goals, 80–90
    resetting of expectations and,
    74–76
    risk allocation and, 132–33
    zero discounting and converting
    goals into cash flow and, 122,
    124–25, 126*f*, 127, 202n
return on investments
    inaccurate perceptions of, 10–11

inflation and, 9, 10, 33, 35, 40,
   97, 111
underperformance and, 9–10
reversion to mean
   rates of return and, 26–27, 111
   real estate values and, 41
   Yale University portfolio and,
      166
"Rich Plus" lifestyle, in retirement,
   76
Rise and Decline of the Medici Bank:
   1397–1494, The (de Roover),
   143
risk
   active management and risk aver-
      sion, 148
   allocating in objective-driven
      investing, 128, 130–33, 131*f*
   Berkshire Hathaway and alloca-
      tion of, 177, 177*f*, 179
   event risk and cash flow and,
      89–90
   external adverse events and,
      87–91
   Forbes 400 list and idiosyncratic
      risk, 66–67
   index funds and, 110–12
   over human lifetimes, 32–33
   private businesses and, 104–5
   Prospect Theory and complex
      attitudes toward, 88–89, 92
   risk-return tradeoff dimensions,
      92–94, 93*f*
   volatility as measure of, 87–88
Risk, Uncertainty and Profit (Knight),
   90
risk-adjusted return target, market
   portfolio construction and, 146,
   204*n*
risk and reward, psychology of
ambiguity and, 21–23
   behavioral biases and, 24–26
   herd mentality and, 23–24
   market reversion and, 26–27
Rockefeller, David, 68
Russia, changing economic conditions in, 33–34

safety
   balancing wealth creation with,
      4–5
   as essential retirement goal, 79, 80
   as principal objective of investing,
      91–92
safety risk bucket and portfolio
   asset and liability allocation to,
      94, 95, 96–97, 134
   caution about, 139–40
   difficult-to-classify asset alloca-
      tion and, 103*f*, 106, 109
   importance of, 184
   performance measurement and,
      116–18
   purpose of, 92, 93*f*
   reviewing and rebalancing of,
      136–37, 137*f*
   risk allocation and, 132–33
   value of, 151
   Wealth Allocation snapshot and,
      127
Samuelson, Paul, 14
savings
   calculating rate needed for retire-
      ment, 73–74, 77
   college and, 124, 152
scarcity, real estate values and, 37–38
Schumpeter, Joseph, 36, 47
Security Analysis (Graham and
   Dodd), 174
self-directed investors
   inaccurate perceptions of results,
      10–11
   poor trading decisions of, 11–12,
      190*n*
   underperformance and, 9–10
Shakespeare, William, 143–44
Sharpe ratio, market portfolio construction and, 146, 204*n*
Shefrin, Hersh, 25
shelter, as essential retirement goal,
   79, 80
Shiller, Robert, 38, 39
shortages, speculative bubbles and, 51
Simons, James H., 65
Sky and Water I (Escher), 44, 44*f*

"social bubbles," in Wealth Allocation Framework, 108–9
social networking, 185
Soros, George, 15, 65
"sources of return test," of Wealth Allocation Framework, 136
South Sea bubble, 47
speculative bubbles
    behavioral traps and, 51–53, 52f
    consequences of, 44, 50, 53, 196n
    Dutch tulip bubble, 45–47, 50
    economic dynamics of, 50–51
    herd mentality and, 23–24, 52
    Internet bubble, 35, 48, 49f
    social, economic, and psychological elements of, 43–45
    transportation bubbles, 47–48
    US housing bubble, 49–50
    wealth creation and, 53–54, 196n
stability
    as important retirement goal, 79–80
    as principal objective of investing, 91–92
Standard & Poor's 500 index, 9, 14, 49f
    return compared to Berkshire Hathaway's return, 178, 208n
standard deviation, Markowitz's use of, 141, 203n
standard of living. See living standards
Statman, Meir, 25
Staunton, Mike, 33–34
stocks
    allocated to risk buckets, 98, 105–6, 201n
    options allocated to risk buckets, 97, 98, 105–6, 201n
    price of, and value investing, 175
subjective approach, to risk allocation, 128
superiority, illusion of
    speculative bubbles and, 53
    in trading, 11
supply and demand, speculative bubbles and, 50–51
Surowiecki, James, 150

"sustainability test," of Wealth Allocation Framework, 135
Swan, Annalyn, 63–64, 68
Swensen, David, 112, 159, 163, 165–66, 180, 205n

Taleb, Nassim Nicholas, 90–91
tax-aware investing, rebalancing and, 145, 152, 154
taxes, lost returns and, 9
technology crash of 2000, company stocks and, 106
Texas Pacific Group, 65
3-D printing, 185–86
time horizon, risk allocation and, 131–32
time periods, average returns across, 151–52, 151f
Tobin, James, 166, 199–200n
"Trading Is Hazardous to Your Wealth" (Barber and Odean), 12
transportation bubbles, 47–48
Treasury bonds, 97, 98
Treasury inflation-protected securities, 97
Triumph of the Optimists: 101 Years of Global Investment Returns (Dimson, Marsh, and Staunton), 33–34
Trump, Donald, 66
tulip bulb bubble, 45–47, 50
Tversky, Amos, 24–25, 88–89, 192n
two-fund theorem, in finance, 199–200n

uncertainty
    behavior and financial decisions and, 24
    bubbles and, 47
    distinguished from risk, 90
    distinguished from volatility, 141, 203n
    Mandelbrot and Knight and, 91, 92, 94
    retirement planning and, 77
    Wealth Allocation Framework and, 92

United States
changing economic conditions in, 33–34, 35–37
fiber-optic bubble in, 48
housing bubble in, 49–50
unequal distribution of wealth in, 57–62, 58–59f, 61f, 186
"Utility of Wealth, The" (Marko-witz), 24

value (utility), speculative bubbles and, 50–51
value investing, 159–60
Berkshire Hathaway risk alloca-tion and, 177, 177f, 179
Berkshire Hathaway success and, 14–15
intellectual origins of, 174
principles of, 174–75
Wealth Allocation Frame-work and risk allocation, 161, 176–80, 177f, 205n
Vanguard Group, 14
venture capital funds, allocated to aspirational risk bucket, 98
volatility of markets
changes in company fortunes, 36
changes in national fortunes, 31, 33–36
human advancement and length-ened lifetimes, 31–32
market portfolio and, 150–51
as measure of risk, 87–88
real estate value changes and, 37–41, 39f
risks over time, 32–33
uncertainty distinguished from, 141, 203n

Wall Street Journal, active manage-ment versus dart-throwing investing, 16–18
wealth
balancing wealth creation with safety, 4–5
common sources of, 63–66
investment strategies and, 66–70

need for strategy to preserve and, 62–63
speculative bubbles and, 53–54, 196n
typical goals for wealthy couple, 123f
unequal US distribution of, 57–62, 58–59f, 61f, 186
see also retirement planning
Wealth Allocation Framework, 4–5
Endowment model of investing and risk allocation, 161, 164–74, 173f, 179–80, 207n
objective-driven steps and snap-shot of, 127–28, 129f, 130f
performance measurement and, 116–18
principal investment objectives of, 91–92
risk buckets and, 92–98, 93f, 101–16, 103f
step 1, outline goals, 122, 123f
step 2, convert goals into cash flow, 122, 124, 125, 126f, 127, 202n
step 3, create Wealth Allocation snapshot, 127–28, 129f, 130f
step 4, assess risk allocation, 128, 130–33, 131f
step 5, allocate assets and diversify portfolio, 134
step 6, analyze and test for stress, 134–36
step 7, review and rebalance, 136–37, 137f
stress tests of, 134–36
value and insights of, 183–87
value investing and, 161, 176–80, 177f, 205n
see also objective-driven investing
weiji (crisis), 43, 43f
Winfrey, Oprah, 65
"wisdom of crowds," market portfo-lio and, 150
Wisdom of Crowds, The (Surowiecki), 150

Yale University, 112, 149
   endowment growth (2000–2009),
     159, 162, 162*f*
   manager selection and, 168–69,
     207n
   policies and portfolio of, 163–64,
     165*f*
   2008 financial crisis and endow-
     ment of, 160–61, 169, 170*f*,
     171–72, 205n
young couple, typical goals for, 123*f*

Zaharoff, Lex, 68–69
Zell, Sam, 66
zero discounting
   converting cash flow into goals
     and, 122, 124–25, 126*f*, 127,
     202n
   retirement planning and, 81–84
zero-sum game
active management as, 12, 147
   markets as, 16
Zhu, Kevin, 12

About the Author

Ashvin B. Chhabra is the chief investment officer of Merrill Lynch Wealth Management, Bank of America. Merrill Lynch is one of the world's largest brokerage and wealth management firms, with over $2 trillion in client balances. Prior to his current position, he was chief investment officer at the Institute of Advanced Study in Princeton, New Jersey. He is widely recognized as one of the founders of goals-based wealth management and for his seminal work "Beyond Markowitz," which integrates modern portfolio theory with behavioral finance. Ashvin grew up in New Delhi and received his PhD in applied physics, in the field of chaos theory, from Yale University, where he also met his Italian-born wife, Daniela Bonafede-Chhabra. He resides in Princeton with his wife, their daughter, Maya, and son, Sasha.